Improving Essential Vocabulary & Spelling Skills

Second Edition

Lawrence Scheg

This book belongs to :

Name: Marantha Bo-Ung
Street: _____
City: _____ State: ____
Phone: _____

The information above is optional

Blogs/Reading Selection
- *Reading selections*
→ *Click on assign reading selection*
- *Download file*

R J Communications LLC
New York

In cooperation with

Sierra Publishing
South Lake Tahoe, California

ISBN: 0-9742756-7-0 and ISBN13: 978-09742756-7-3

Published by
R J Communications
51 East 42nd Street, Suite 1202
New York, NY 10017

In cooperation with
Sierra Publishing
South Lake Tahoe, CA 96150

Contact for Domestic and International Orders:
Send E-mail to: mailsierrapublishing@yahoo.com
or visit www.SierraPublishing.com

Printed in the United States of America

5th printing

Contents:

Plus … This edition contains a CD Rom that includes: The entire Vocabulary book in e-book format, ReadPlease © software, interactive puzzles, audio practice tests, and printable study cards containing the vocabulary word, and letter grouped vocabulary word, on one side, and the definition on the reverse.

How to Set Up Your Computer for Using the Interactive Puzzles

1. Open your C drive and find the folder labeled "Programs".
2. Open the "Programs" folder.
3. Find the folder labeled "Internet Explorer" and open it.
4. Make the window' box smaller by dragging the sides to form a smaller view.
5. Now locate the drive containing your *Advancing College Vocabulary & Spelling Skills* CD and find the folder labeled "Puzzle Software."
6. Open that folder, create a smaller window and place it next to the "Internet Explorer" window,
7. Choose "Select all" from the edit menu for the "Puzzle Software", and then drag all of the highlighted files over into the "Internet Explorer" folder.
8. Close all windows.
9. You are now ready to use the interactive puzzles on the disk. Open your *Advancing College Vocabulary & Spelling Skills* CD and find the folder labeled "Interactive Puzzles."
10. Click on the blue Internet Explorer **E** files relating to the chapter puzzle that you want to do. The puzzle should now appear and be ready for your use. The contents of the "Interactive Puzzles" folder may also be copied to a folder on your C drive. Simply create a new folder, label it "interactive Puzzles," and (as above) drag and drop **ALL** of the **puzzle files** into that folder.

Acknowledgements:

Photography Courtesy of:

Cover: Copyright © Lawrence Scheg

Chapter 1: Copyright © Lawrence Scheg

Chapter 2: Copyright © Nathan & Danielle Scheg

Chapter 3: Copyright © Lawrence Scheg

Chapter 4: Copyright © Lawrence Scheg

Chapter 5: Copyright © Lawrence Scheg

Chapter 6: Copyright © Lawrence Scheg

Chapter 7: Courtesy of NASA

Chapter 8: Courtesy of NASA

Chapter 9: Copyright © Lawrence Scheg

Chapter 10: Copyright © Lawrence Scheg

Chapter 11: Copyright © Lawrence Scheg

Chapter 12: Copyright © Lawrence Scheg

Chapter 13: Courtesy of NASA

Chapter 14: Copyright © Lawrence Scheg

Chapter 15: Copyright © Lawrence Scheg

Chapter 16: Copyright © Lawrence Scheg

Chapter 17: Copyright © Lawrence Scheg

Chapter 18: Copyright © Lawrence Scheg

Chapter 19: Copyright © Lawrence Scheg

Chapter 20: Copyright © Lawrence Scheg

How to use the Audio Practice Tests

1. Put your disk into the CD drive of your computer.
2. Click on "My Computer" on your desktop.
3. You will now see "IEV&SS-SCHEG"
4. Click on that disk.
5. When it opens, find the folder "Audio Practice Tests" and click on it.
6. Find the chapter or page number that corresponds to the words that you want to hear and click on that file.
7. The Audio Practice Tests will open in virtually any audio program that is installed on your computer.
8. You may now hear the words pronounced. You may "pause" the word dictation, "reverse" to repeat a word, or "play" as many times as you'd like.
9. The Audio Practice Tests may be used to learn the proper pronunciation of the words, or you may test yourself on their proper spelling. Simply write the words on a sheet of paper as they are dictated and then turn to the proper page (as directed at the end of each test) to correct your answers.

Improving Essential Vocabulary and Spelling Skills

I.)   ***Reflect and Connect:*** Complete the following sentences with words that are **familiar** to you and that make sense in each sentence. You may write more than one word choice for each blank space. **Do not** look at or study the new words yet. Answers will vary and your instructor will discuss them with you.

adamant   **1.** She was very ___adamant___ that the Mitsubishi Eclipse would be her next new car.

adapt   **2.** The dog was moved to the desert where it had to ___adapt___ to its hot new environment.

adhere   **3.** At the police academy, all officers must ___follow___ to the rules.

adjacent   **4.** Old Highway road runs ___next___ to the Highway 210.

adverse   **5.** After Lori took her new medication, she had ___the opposite___ reactions and needed to be hospitalized.

advocate   **6.** John is a(n) ___supporter___ for animal rights, and therefore does not eat meat.

debilitate   **7.** Diabetes can ___weaken___ an individual if proper medication is not taken.

delaration   **8.** Thomas Jefferson wrote a(n) ___declaration___ stating the reasons for the United States wishing to sever ties with Great Britain.

deduction   **9.** The IRS allows a certain amount of ___numbers___ for small businesses.

default   **10.** If you do not make your mortgage payments, it will cause a ___debt___ on your loan.

defect   **11.** Henry had a slight speech ___issue___, but he was able to overcome it and pursued a career in public speaking.

deficient   **12.** Anemia is a condition in which a person is ___lack___ in iron.

demoralize   **13.** The terrorist attack was intended to ___eliminate___ the people.

enumeration   **14.** A(n) ___finding___ of the number of 9/11 victims took several months.

deteriorate   **15.** Many women take a calcium supplement so that their bones will not ___break apart___.

II.) ***Study the words and definitions below.*** These words and definitions are also on the enclosed CD Rom and may be printed out as study cards. The words are broken into letter groupings for easier spelling. Also, that is followed by a common definition, and common forms of the word that you might encounter. Your instructor will pronounce the words for you or you may want to use an audio dictionary for more help.

1. **adamant (ad/a/mant)** 1. Strong in opinion. 2. having the qualities of adamant; that cannot be broken, dissolved, or penetrated, as adamantine bonds, or chains.
2. **adapt (ad/apt)** 1. To make suitable. 2. To fit or suit.
3. **adhere (ad/here)** 1. To stick to, as glutinous substances, or by natural growth. 2. To be joined, or held in contact; to cleave to. 3. Figuratively, to hold to, be attached, or remain fixed, either by personal union or conformity of faith, principle, or opinion; as, people adhere to a party, a leader, a church, or creed. 4. To be consistent; to hold together as the parts of a system.
4. **adjacent (ad/ja/cent)** 1. Lying near, close, or contiguous; bordering upon. 2. next to
5. **adverse (ad/ver/se)** 1. Opposite; opposing; acting in a contrary direction; conflicting. 2. Figuratively, opposing desire; contrary to the wishes, or to supposed good; hence, unfortunate; calamitous; afflictive; pernicious, unprosperous; as, adverse fate or circumstances.
6. **advocate (ad/vo/cate)** 1. (n) one who supports a cause. 2. To plead in favor of; to defend by argument before a tribunal; 3. To support or vindicate.
7. **debilitate (de/bil/i/tate)** To weaken; to impair the strength of; to enfeeble; to make faint; to exhaust.
8. **declaration (de/clar/a/tion)** 1. An affirmation; an open expression of facts or opinions; verbal utterance. 2. Expression of facts, opinions, promises, predictions in writings; records or reports of what has been declared or uttered. 3. Publication; manifestation; 4. A public annunciation; proclamation; as the Declaration of Independence, July 4, 1776. 5. In law, that part of the process or pleadings in which the plaintiff sets forth at large his cause of complaint; the narration or count.

9. **deduction (de/duc/tion)** 1. The act of deducting. 2. That which is deducted; sum or amount taken from another; abatement; as, this sum is a deduction from the yearly rent. 3. That which is drawn from premises; fact, opinion, or hypothesis, collected from principles or facts stated, or established data; inference; consequence drawn; conclusion; as, this opinion is a fair deduction from the principles you have advanced.

10. **default (de/fau/lt)** 1. To fail in performing a contract or agreement. 2. A failing, or failure; an omission of that which ought to be done; neglect to do what duty or law requires. 3. In law, a failure of appearance in court at a day assigned, particularly of the defendant in a suit when called to make answer. It may be applied to jurors, witnesses, etc.; but a plaintiffs' failing to appear by himself or attorney, is usually called a non-appearance. 4. To suffer default, is to permit an action to be called without appearing or answering; applied to a defendant.

11. **defect (de/fect)** 1. Want or absence of something necessary or useful towards perfection; fault; imperfection. 2. Failing; fault; mistake; imperfection in moral conduct, or in judgment. 3. Any want, or imperfection, in natural objects; the absence of any thing necessary to perfection; any thing unnatural or misplaced; blemish; deformity.

12. **deficient de/fi/ci/ent)** 1. Wanting; defective; imperfect; not sufficient or adequate; as deficient estate; deficient strength. 2. Wanting; not having a full or adequate supply.

13. **demoralize (de/mor/al/ize)** 1. To corrupt or undermine the morals of. 2. To destroy or lessen the effect of moral principles on. To render corrupt in morals. To take away from a person's self-worth.

14. **enumeration e/num/er/a/tion)** 1. An account of a number of things, in which mention is made of every particular article. 2. In rhetoric, a part of a peroration, in which the orator recapitulates the principal points or heads of the discourse or argument.

15. **deteriorate (de/ter/ior/ate)** To grow worse; to be impaired in quality to degenerate.

III.) *Match the words with their definitions.* Draw a line from the word in the first column to the definition in the second column.

j. 1. adamant
m. 2. adapt
f. 3. adhere
h. 4. adjacent
e. 5. adverse
d. 6. advocate
n. 7. debilitate
l. 8. declaration
o. 9. deduction
a. 10. default
c. 11. defect
g. 12. deficient
i. 13. demoralize
k. 14. enumeration
b. 15. deteriorate

a. not paying as agreed
b. to fall apart
c. an imperfection
d. a supporter
e. working against, not good
f. to stick to
g. not enough
h. next to
i. take a person's self-worth
j. strong in opinion
k. counting
l. statement of reasons
m. to fit in
n. to exhaust all energy
o. to lessen, reduce, or subtract

IV.) *Puzzle work.* Now try the interactive puzzle. Put the CD (that came with your workbook) into the computer, and work the puzzle. A paper copy of the puzzle is also included at the end of this chapter.

V.)   Write the correct new word in each sentence below:

adapt	adjacent	adverse	adamant	adhere
debilitate	deduction	default	advocate	declaration
deficient	enumeration	deteriorate	defect	demoralize

1. She was very ___adamant___ that the Mitsubishi Eclipse would be her next new car.
2. The dog was moved to the desert where it had to ___adapt___ to its hot new environment.
3. At the police academy, all officers must ___adhere___ to the rules.
4. Old Highway road runs ___adjacent___ to the Highway 210.
5. After Lori took her new medication, she had ___adverse___ reactions and needed to be hospitalized.
6. John is a(n) ___advocate___ for animal rights, and therefore does not eat meat.
7. Diabetes can ___debilitate___ an individual if proper medication is not taken.
8. Thomas Jefferson wrote a(n) ___declaration___ stating the reasons for the United States wishing to sever ties with Great Britain.
9. The IRS allows a certain amount of ___deduction___ for small businesses.
10. If you do not make your mortgage payments, it will cause a(n) ___default___ on your loan.
11. Henry had a slight speech ___defect___, but he was able to overcome it and pursued a career in public speaking.
12. Anemia is a condition in which a person is ___deficient___ in iron.
13. The terrorist attack was intended to ___demoralize___ the people.
14. A(n) ___enumeration___ of the number of 9/11 victims took several months.
15. Many women take a calcium supplement so that their bones will not ___deteriorate___.

VI.) Are you ready to take the practice test? You may take the practice test as many times as you want to. Simply insert the CD that came with book into your computer, go to "My Computer", open the CD by clicking on it, find the Practice test folder, choose this chapter's practice test and begin. (You will need a sheet of paper to write your answers on.) When finished, turn back to this chapter and correct your test. The answers are in the same order as exercise II.

VII.) Are you ready to use the new words? Write a sentence for each new word.

adamant	adhere	adverse	adapt	adjacent
advocate	declaration	default	debilitate	deduction
defect	demoralize	deteriorate	deficient	enumeration

1. _____

2. _____

3. _____

4. _____

5. _____

6. _____

7. _____

8. _____

9. _____

10. _____

11. _____

12. _____

13. _____

14. _____

15. _____

VIII.) Your instructor may ask you to do the puzzle on the next page. It is the same as the one on your CD. You are able to do it here once or on the CD as many times as you'd like.

Across

1. to exhaust all energy

3. not paying as agreed

6. to stick to

7. strong in opinion

9. counting

10. to lessen or reduce; subtraction

11. an imperfection

12. not enough

Down

2. to fit in

3. statement of reasons for doing something

4. to fall apart

5. take away a person's self-worth

6. working against, not good for

8. a supporter

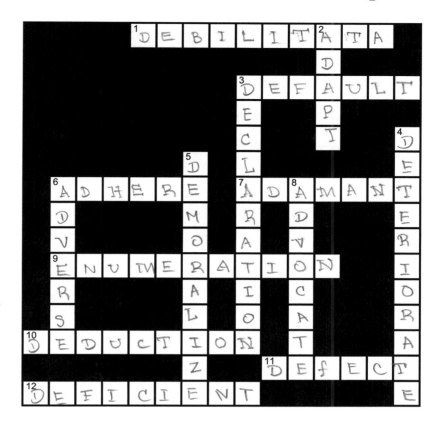

Rewrite your words

New word:		Practice writing the new word:		
Adamant				
Adept				
Adhere				
Adjacent				
Adverse				
Advocate				
debilitate				
declaration				
deduction				
default				
defect				
deficient				
demoralize				
enumeration				
deteriorate				

Improving Essential Vocabulary and Spelling Skills

I.)   *Reflect and Connect:* Complete the following sentences with words that are **familiar** to you and that make sense in each sentence. You may write more than one word choice for each blank space. **Do not** look at or study the new words yet. Answers will vary and your instructor will discuss them with you.

delineate   1. Sometimes it's good to ___go through___ every step of a plan so that everyone is clear concerning their part in it.

delusion   2. Mike is under a(n) ___illusion___ in thinking he can get through college without studying.

demise   3. Lying excessively led to her ___downfall___.

denounce   4. The politician had to ___announce___ all affiliation with foreign campaign money.

desecrate   5. Vandals sometimes ___vandalize___ graves with spray paint.

designate   6. In our office, I was to ___order___ each person with a specific job to do.

destiny   7. Some say it was ___love___ that led them to their romantic partner.

deterrent   8. The cones on the freeway are a(n) ___signs___ to warn of construction ahead.

detrimental   9. It is ___a loss___ to your grades if you do not study before a test.

devestated   10. The earthquake ___shook___ the town.

deviate   11. The city council began to ___turn away___ from the main topic and began to talk about a new issue.

devious   12. He was a(n) ___a terrible___ salesperson who was selling other people's property without their consent.

devise   13. She began to ___organize___ a plan to save the forest land.

devoid   14. The sky was pitch black and ___absense___ of any stars.

dispatch   15. The police ___officer___ showed up in a matter of minutes at the crime scene.

II.) ***Study the words and definitions below.*** These words and definitions are also on the enclosed CD Rom and may be printed out as study cards. The words are broken into letter groupings for easier spelling. Also, that is followed by a common definition, and common forms of the word that you might encounter. Your instructor will pronounce the words for you or you may want to use an audio dictionary for more help.

1. **delineate (de/lin/e/ate)** 1. To draw the lines which exhibit the form of a thing; to mark out with lines; to sketch; to diagram. 2. To paint; to represent in picture; to draw a likeness of. 3. Figuratively, to describe; to represent to the mind or understanding; to exhibit a likeness in words. 4. To explain in detail.
2. **delusion (de/lus/ion)** 1. The act of deluding; deception; a misleading of the mind. 2. False representation; illusion; error or mistake proceeding from false views; not having to do with reality
3. **demise (de/mise)** 1. Death; 2. Serious downfall
4. **denounce (de/noun/ce)** 1. To declare solemnly; to proclaim in a threatening manner; to announce or declare, as a threat. 2. To threaten by some outward sign, or expression. 3. To inform against; to accuse; to speak against.
5. **desecrate (de/se/cr/ate)** 1. To divert from a sacred purpose. 2. to damage something considered holy.
6. **designate (de/sig/nate)** 1. To mark out or show, so as to make known; to indicate by visible lines, marks, description or something known and determinate; 2. To point out; to distinguish from others by indication. 3. To appoint; to select or distinguish for a particular purpose; to assign.
7. **destiny (des/tiny)** 1. State or condition appointed or predetermined; ultimate fate. 2. Invincible necessity; fate; a necessity or fixed order of things established by a divine decree, or by an indissoluble connection of causes and effects.

8. **deterrent (de/terr/ent)** Something that gets in the way
9. **detrimental (de/tri/men/tal)** Injurious; hurtful; causing loss or damage.
10. **devastate (de/vas/tate)** To lay waste; to waste; to ravage; to utterly destroy.
11. **deviate (de/vi/ate)** 1. To turn aside or wander from the common or right way, course or line, either in a literal or figurative sense. 2. To stray from the path of duty; to wander, in a moral sense; to err; to sin.
12. **devious (de/vi/ous)** 1. Out of the common way or track; as a devious course. 2. Wandering; roving; rambling. 3. Erring; going astray from rectitude or the divine precepts; inclined to evil action.
13. **devise (de/vise)** 1. To invent; to contrive; to form in the mind by new combinations of ideas, new applications of principles, or new arrangement of parts; to plan; to scheme; to project; to create
14. **devoid (de/void)** 1. Void; empty; vacant. 2. Destitute; not possessing; without, lacking. 3. Free from.
15. **dispatch (dis/pat/ch)** 1. To send or send away; particularly applied to the sending of messengers, agents and letters on special business, and often implying haste. 2. To send out of the world; to put to death. 3. To perform; to execute speedily; to finish; as, the business was dispatched in due time. 4. To conclude an affair with another; to transact and finish. 5. Speedy performance; execution or transaction of business with due diligence. 6. Speed; haste; expedition; due diligence. 7. A letter sent or to be sent with expedition, by a messenger express; or a letter on some affair of state, or of public concern; or a packet of letters, sent by some public officer, on public business.

III.) ***Match the words with their definitions.*** Draw a line from the word in the first column to the definition in the second column.

i. 1. delineate
e. 2. delusion
m. 3. demise
j. 4. denounce
o. 5. desecrate
l. 6. designate
n. 7. destiny
c. 8. deterrent
d. 9. detrimental
a. 10. devastate
  11. deviate
f. 12. devious
k. 13. devise
g. 14. devoid
h. 15. dispatch

a. to destroy
b. to turn away from
c. something gets in the way
d. not good for you
e. not reality
f. inclined to evil action
g. without
h. to send
i. to explain in detail
j. to speak against
k. to create
l. to appoint
m. death
n. fate
o. destroy something holy

IV.) ***Puzzle work.*** Now try the interactive puzzle. Put the CD (that came with your workbook) into the computer, and work the puzzle. A paper copy of the puzzle is also included at the end of this chapter.

V.) **Write the correct new word in each sentence below:**

delineate	delusion	demise	denounce	desecrate
designate	destiny	deterrent	detrimental	devastate
deviate	devious	devise	devoid	dispatch

1. Sometimes it's good to ___delineate___ every step of a plan so that everyone is clear concerning their part in it.
2. Mike is under a(n) ___delusion___ in thinking he can get through college without studying.
3. Lying excessively led to her ___demise___ .
4. The politician had to ___declare___ all affiliation with foreign campaign money.
5. Vandals sometimes ___desecrate___ graves with spray paint.
6. In our office, I was to ___designate___ each person with a specific job to do.
7. Some say it was ___destiny___ that led them to their romantic partner.
8. The cones on the freeway are a(n) ___deterrent___ to warn of construction ahead.
9. It is ___detrimental___ to your grades if you do not study before a test.
10. The earthquake ___devastate___ the town.
11. The city council began to ___deviate___ from the main topic and began to talk about a new issue.
12. He was a(n) ___devious___ salesperson who was selling other people's property without their consent.
13. She began to ___devise___ a plan to save the forest land.
14. The sky was pitch black and ___devoid___ of any stars.
15. The police ___dispatch___ showed up in a matter of minutes at the crime scene.

VI.) Are you ready to take the practice test? You may take the practice test as many times as you want to. Simply insert the CD that came with book into your computer, go to "My Computer", open the CD by clicking on it, find the Practice test folder, choose this chapter's practice test and begin. (You will need a sheet of paper to write your answers on.) When finished, turn back to this chapter and correct your test. The answers are in the same order as exercise II.

VII.) Are you ready to use the new words? Write a sentence for each new word.

delineate	delusion	demise	denounce	desecrate
designate	destiny	deterrent	detrimental	devastate
deviate	devious	devise	devoid	dispatch

1. _____

_____

2. _____

_____

3. _____

_____

4. _____

_____

5. _____

_____

6. _____

_____

7. _____

_____

8. _____

_____

9. _____

_____

10. _____

_____

11. _____

_____

12. _____

_____

13. _____

_____

14. _____

_____

15. _____

_____

VIII.) Your instructor may ask you to do the puzzle on the next page. It is the same as the one on your CD. You are able to do it here once or on the CD as many times as you'd like.

Across

2. to damage something holy

3. death

5. to explain in detail

6. to appoint

8. inclined to evil action

9. fate

10. to destroy

Down

1. without; empty

2. to send

3. not having to do with reality

4. something that gets in the way

6. to turn away from

7. to speak against

8. to create

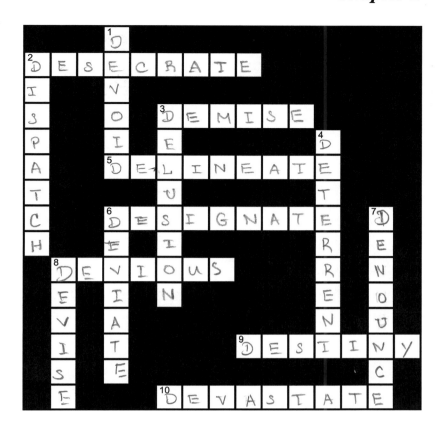

Rewrite your words

New word:		Practice writing the new word:		

Improving Essential Vocabulary and Spelling Skills

I.) **Reflect and Connect:** Complete the following sentences with words that are **familiar** to you and that make sense in each sentence. You may write more than one word choice for each blank space. **Do not** look at or study the new **words yet.** Answers will vary and your instructor will discuss them with you.

discern   **1. Mario is able to** ___pick out___ **right from wrong.**

disclose   **2. It is illegal to** ___view___ **some information before a trial.**

discipline   **3. It takes great** ___training___ **to do well in life.**

discrepancy   **4. There was a(n)** ___arguement___ **as to who hit the blue car first.**

discriminate **5. You shouldn't** ___distinguish___ **against people of other races.**

disdain   **6. The terrorist felt the** ___discust___ **of the people for his evil actions.**

dismal   **7. It was a foggy and very** ___gloomy___ **day.**

dismay   **8. The turnout for the march was low and caused some** ___sadness___ **among the supporters of the initiative.**

disparage **9. Dennis began to** ___interupt___ **Amanda's statement before she even finished.**

dispassionate **10. The novel was a(n)** ___moderate___ **piece without any true emotion.**

dispel   **11. She said, "let me** ___stop___ **any rumors - there is no one involved in this but me."**

dispense   **12. In the famine, the troops were to** ___seperate___ **rations to all civilians.**

disperse   **13. The troops ordered the unruly crowd to** ___spread___ **.**

dissent   **14. There was much** ___issue___ **over the formation of a new Government.**

dissonance **15. The people could not agree on very much, so a period of great** ___disagrement___ **prevailed.**

II.) *Study the words and definitions below.* These words and definitions are also on the enclosed CD Rom and may be printed out as study cards. The words are broken into letter groupings for easier spelling. Also, that is followed by a common definition, and common forms of the word that you might encounter. Your instructor will pronounce the words for you or you may want to use an audio dictionary for more help.

1. **discern (dis/cern)** 1. To separate by the eye, or by the understanding. 2. To distinguish; to see the difference between two or more things; to discriminate. 3. To discover; to see; to distinguish by the eye. 4. To discover by the intellect; to distinguish; hence, to have knowledge of; to judge.

2. **disclose (dis/close)** 1. To uncover; to open; to remove a cover from, and lay open to the view. 2. To discover; to lay open to the view; to bring to light. 3. To reveal by words; to tell; to utter. 4. To make known; to show in any manner.

3. **discipline (dis/ci/pline)** 1. Education; instruction; cultivation and improvement, correct sentiments, morals and manners, and due subordination to authority. 2. Method of regulating principles and practice. 3. Subjection to laws, rules, order, precepts or regulations. 4. Correction; chastisement; punishment intended to correct crimes or errors. 5. To instruct or educate; to inform the mind; to prepare by instructing in correct principles and habits. 6. To instruct and govern; to teach rules and practice, and accustom to order and subordination; as, to discipline troops or an army. 7. To advance and prepare by instruction; focused training.

4. **discrepancy (dis/cre/pan/cy)** to show an inconsistency; difference; disagreement.

5. **discriminate (dis/crim/in/ate)** 1. To make a difference or distinction; as, in the application of law, and the punishment of crimes. 2. To observe or note a difference; to distinguish; as, in judging of evidence. 3. To distinguish; to observe the difference between. 4. To separate; to select from others; to make a distinction between. 5. To mark with notes of difference; to distinguish by some note or mark. 6. To be prejudiced.

6. **disdain (dis/dain)** To think unworthy; to deem worthless; to consider to be unworthy of notice, care, regard, esteem, or unworthy of ones character; to scorn; to condemn; to despise

7. **dismal (dis/mal)** 1. Dark; gloomy. 2. Sorrowful; dire; horrid; melancholy; calamitous; unfortunate. 3. Frightful; horrible.

8. **dismay (dis/may)** 1. Fall or loss of courage; a sinking of the spirits; depression; dejection; a yielding to fear; that loss of firmness which is effected by fear or terror; fear impressed; terror felt. 2. To deprive of that strength or firmness of mind which constitutes courage; to discourage; to dishearten; to sink or depress the spirits or resolution; apprehension.

9. **disparage (dis/par/age)** To treat with contempt; to undervalue; to lower in rank or estimation; to vilify; to bring reproach on; to reproach; to debase by words or actions; to dishonor; to ignore as unimportant.

10. **dispassionate (dis/pass/ion/ate)** 1. Free from passion; calm; composed; impartial; moderate; temperate; unmoved by feelings.

11. **dispel (dis/pel)** To scatter by driving or force; to disperse; to dissipate; to banish; to get rid of.

12. **dispense (dis/pen/se)** 1. To deal or divide out in parts or portions; to distribute; to give out. 2. To administer; to apply, as laws to particular cases; to distribute justice. 3. To permit not to take effect; to neglect or pass by; to suspend the operation or application of something required, established or customary. 4. To excuse from; to give leave not to do or observe what is required or commanded. 5. To do without.

13. **disperse (dis/per/se) .** To scatter; to drive asunder; to cause to separate into different parts. 2. To diffuse; to spread.   3. To dissipate. 4. To distribute.

14. **dissent (diss/ent)** 1. To disagree in opinion; to differ; to think in a different or contrary manner. 2. To show disagreement.

15. **dissonance (diss/on/an/ce)** 1. Discord; a mixture or union of harsh, unharmonious sounds, which are grating or unpleasing to the ear. 2. Disagreement of sounds; disharmony.

III.) *Match the words with their definitions.* Draw a line from the word in the first column to the definition in the second column.

f. 1. discern
h. 2. disclose
n. 3. discipline
i 4. discrepancy
j 5. discriminate
o 6. disdain
7. dismal
8. dismay
g 9. disparage
10. dispassionate
k 11. dispel
12. dispense
a 13. disperse
d 14. dissent
c 15. dissonance

a. to scatter
b. conflicting
c. disharmony
d. to strongly disagree
e. to give out
f. to know the difference
g. to ignore as unimportant
h. to reveal
i. to show an inconsistency
j. to be prejudiced
k. to get rid of
l. unfortunate
m. to create apprehension
n. focused training
o. to despise

IV.) *Puzzle work.* Now try the interactive puzzle. Put the CD (that came with your workbook) into the computer, and work the puzzle. A paper copy of the puzzle is also included at the end of this chapter.

V.) **Write the correct new word in each sentence below:**

discern	disclose	discipline	discrepancy	discriminate
disdain	dismal	dismay	disparage	dispassionate
dispel	dispense	disperse	dissent	dissonance

1. Mario is able to ___discern___ right from wrong.
2. It is illegal to ___disclose__ some information before a trial.
3. It takes great ___discipline___ to do well in life.
4. There was a(n) ___discrepancy___ as to who hit the blue car first.
5. You shouldn't ___discriminat___ against people of other races.
6. The terrorist felt the ___disdain___ of the people for his evil actions.
7. It was a foggy and very ___dismal___ day.
8. The turnout for the march was low and caused some ___dismay___ among the supporters of the initiative.
9. Dennis began to ___disparage___ Amanda's statement before she even finished.
10. The novel was a(n) ___dispasionat___ piece without any true emotion.
11. She said, "let me ___dispel___ any rumors - there is no one involved in this but me."
12. In the famine, the troops were to ___dispense___ rations to all civilians.
13. The troops ordered the unruly crowd to ___disperse___.
14. There was much ___dissent___ over the formation of a new Government.
15. The people could not agree on very much, so a period of great ___dissonance___ prevailed.

VI.) **Are you ready to take the practice test?** You may take the practice test as many times as you want to. Simply insert the CD that came with book into your computer, go to "My Computer", open the CD by clicking on it, find the Practice test folder, choose this chapter's practice test and begin. (You will need a sheet of paper to write your answers on.) When finished, turn back to this chapter and correct your test. The answers are in the same order as exercise II.

VII.) Are you ready to use the new words? Write a sentence for each new word.

discern	disclose	discipline	discrepancy	discriminate
disdain	dismal	dismay	disparage	dispassionate
dispel	dispense	disperse	dissent	dissonance

1. _____

2. _____

3. _____

4. _____

5. _____

6. _____

7. _____

8. _____

9. _____

10. _____

11. _____

12. _____

13. _____

14. _____

15. _____

VIII.) Your instructor may ask you to do the puzzle on the next page. It is the same as the one on your CD. You are able to do it here once or on the CD as many times as you'd like.

Across

1. apprehension

5. to give out

8. unfortunate; bleak

9. to show disagreement

10. to be prejudiced

11. focused training

Down

1. to scatter

2. to know the difference

3. calm, unmoved

4. to reveal

6. to get rid of

7. conflict, discord

8. to ignore as unimportant

9. to despise

Rewrite your words

New word:		Practice writing the new word:		
Discern				
Disclose				
Discipline				
Discrepancy				
Discriminate				
Disdain				
dismal				
Dismay				
Disparage				
Dispassionate				
Dispel				
Dispense				
Disperse				
Dissent				
Dissonance				

Improving Essential Vocabulary and Spelling Skills

I.) *Reflect and Connect:* Complete the following sentences with words that are **familiar** to you and that make sense in each sentence. You may write more than one word choice for each blank space. **<u>Do not</u> look at or study the new words yet.** Answers will vary and your instructor will discuss them with you.

concede **1. None of the candidates wanted to** ___admit___ **their loss to the winners.**

conceive **2. Many infertile couples try various methods to** ___have___ **a child.**

conciliatory **3. There was a(n)** ___conflicting___ **tone at the meeting as the two enemies decided to work towards peace.**

concise **4. The doctor left clear and** ___precise___ **directions for the nurse.**

concurrent **5. The** ___meeting___ **times of the afternoon sporting events caused us to have to program our Tivo recorder.**

condescending **6. The young boy got in trouble for using a(n)** ___imature___ **tone with his mother.**

condone **7. I would never** ___accept___ **bad behavior.**

conducive **8. The lit candles in the room made the atmosphere** ___right___ **to romance.**

confiscate **9. The police were able to** ___catch___ **illegal drugs during the traffic stop.**

congenial **10. Everyone was very** ___friendly___ **at their first meeting.**

consecutive **11. The New York Yankees won five** ___consecutive___ **games and that allowed them to play in the World Series.**

consensus **12. There was a(n)** ___agreement___ **among the players that they could win the championship.**

consequence **13. One** ___outcom___ **of not learning material thoroughly is an inability to have the proper knowledge later in life when it is needed.**

contiguous **14. There are forty-eight** ___joining___ **states that make up the mainland of the United States.**

constrict **15. An allergy attack can sometimes** ___bring forth___ **a person's airway resulting in a condition called anaphylactic shock.**

II.) ***Study the words and definitions below.*** These words and definitions are also on the enclosed CD Rom and may be printed out as study cards. The words are broken into letter groupings for easier spelling. Also, that is followed by a common definition, and common forms of the word that you might encounter. Your instructor will pronounce the words for you or you may want to use an audio dictionary for more help.

1. **concede (con/cede)** 1. To yield; to admit as true, just or proper; to grant; to let pass undisputed. 2. To allow.
2. **conceive (con/cei/ve)** 1. To form in the mind; to imagine; to devise. 2. To form an idea in the mind; to understand; to comprehend. 3. To think; to be of opinion; to have an idea. 4. To receive into the womb, and breed; to begin the formation of the embryo or fetus of animal.
3. **conciliatory (con/cil/ia/tory)** Tending to conciliate, or reconcile; tending to make peace between persons at variance; moving toward a peaceful tone.
4. **concise (con/cise)** Brief; short, applied to language or style; containing few words; comprehensive; comprehending much in a few words; the principal matters only.
5. **concurrent (con/curr/ent)** 1. Meeting; uniting; accompanying; acting in conjunction; agreeing in the same act; contributing to the same event or effect; operating with. 2. Joint and equal; existing together and operating on the same objects; simultaneous.
6. **condescending (con/des/cen/ding)** 1. Yielding to inferiors. 2. Patronizingly superior attitude
7. **condone (con/done)** To lend support to
8. **conducive (con/du/cive)** having a tendency to promote; agreeable, favorable, beneficial, useful.
9. **confiscate (con/fis/cate)** 1. Forfeited and adjudged to the public treasury, as the goods of a criminal. 2. To lawfully take.
10. **congenial (con/gen/ial)** 1. Partaking of the same genus, kind or nature. 2. Belonging to the nature; natural; agreeable to the nature. 3. Adapted. 4. Friendly, harmonious, likeminded.

11. **consecutive (con/sec/u/tive)** Succeeding one another in a regular order; successive; uninterrupted in course or succession.

12. **consensus (con/sen/sus)** Near unanimous agreement; accord.

13. **consequence (con/se/quen/ce)** 1. That which follows from any act, cause, principle, or series of actions. Hence, an event or effect produced by some preceding act or cause. 2. In logic, a proposition collected from the agreement of other previous propositions; the conclusion which results from reason or argument; inference; deduction. 3. Connection of cause and effect. 4. Influence; tendency, as to effects. 5. Importance; extensive influence; distinction.

14. **contiguous (con/tig/u/ous)** Touching; meeting or joining at the surface or border; as two contiguous bodies or countries. Touching without interruption. Touching without intervening space; continuous.

15. **constrict (con/st/rict)** To draw together; to bind; to cramp; to draw into a narrow compass; hence, to contract or cause to shrink. 2. Close down.

III.) *Match the words with their definitions.* Draw a line from the word in the first column to the definition in the second column.

g. 1. concede   a. friendly
h. 2. conceive   b. successive; in order
n. 3. conciliatory   c. shrink; close down
m. 4. concise   d. near unanimous agreement
o. 5. concurrent   e. to lawfully take
k. 6. condescending   f. touching w/o interruption
j. 7. condone   g. give in
l. 8. conducive   h. to think of
e. 9. confiscate   i. a result of an action
f. 10. congenial   j. to lend support to
b. 11. consecutive   k. patronizing attitude
d. 12. consensus   l. agreeable
i. 13. consequence   m. brief and to the point
f. 14. contiguous   n. moving toward peace
c. 15. constrict   o. occurring at the same time

IV.) *Puzzle work.* Now try the interactive puzzle. Put the CD (that came with your workbook) into the computer, and work the puzzle. A paper copy of the puzzle is also included at the end of this chapter.

V.) Write the correct new word in each sentence below:

conceive	conciliatory	concurrent	concede	concise
condone	conducive	congenial	condescending	confiscate
consensus	consequence	constrict	consecutive	contiguous

1. None of the candidates wanted to ___concede___ their loss to the winners.

2. Many infertile couples try various methods to ___conceive___ a child.

3. There was a(n) ___conciliatory___ tone at the meeting as the two enemies decided to work towards peace.

4. The doctor left clear and ___consise___ directions for the nurse.

5. The ___concurrent___ times of the afternoon sporting events caused us to have to program our Tivo recorder.

6. The young boy got in trouble for using a(n) ___condescending___ tone with his mother.

7. I would never ___condone___ bad behavior.

8. The lit candles in the room made the atmosphere ___conducive___ to romance.

9. The police were able to ___confiscate___ illegal drugs during the traffic stop.

10. Everyone was very ___congenial___ at their first meeting.

11. The New York Yankees won five ___consecutive___ games and that allowed them to play in the World Series.

12. There was a(n) ___consensus___ among the players that they could win the championship.

13. One ___consequence___ of not learning material thoroughly is an inability to have the proper knowledge later in life when it is needed.

14. There are forty-eight ___contiguous___ states that make up the mainland of the United States.

15. An allergy attack can sometimes ___constrict___ a person's airway resulting in a condition called anaphylactic shock.

VI.) Are you ready to take the practice test? You may take the practice test as many times as you want to. Simply insert the CD that came with book into your computer, go to "My Computer", open the CD by clicking on it, find the Practice test folder, choose this chapter's practice test and begin. (You will need a sheet of paper to write your answers on.) When finished, turn back to this chapter and correct your test. The answers are in the same order as exercise II.

VII.) Are you ready to use the words? Write a sentence for each word.

concede	conciliatory	concurrent	conceive	concise
condescending	conducive	congenial	condone	confiscate
consecutive	consequence	constrict	consensus	contiguous

1. _____

2. _____

3. _____

4. _____

5. _____

6. _____

7. _____

8. _____

9. _____

10. _____

11. _____

12. _____

13. _____

14. _____

15. _____

VIII.) Your instructor may ask you to do the puzzle on the next page. It is the same as the one on your CD. You are able to do it here once or on the CD as many times as you'd like.

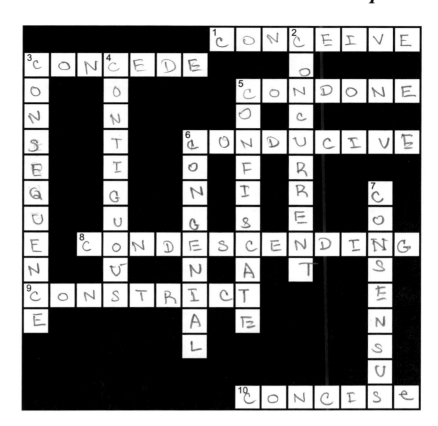

Across

1. to think of; become pregnant

3. give in

5. to lend support to

6. agreeable

8. patronizingly superior attitude

9. shrink; close down

10. brief and to the point

Down

2. happening at the same time

3. a result of an action

4. touching; without interruption

5. to lawfully take

6. friendly

7. near unanimous agreement

Rewrite your words

New word:		Practice writing the new word:		

Improving Essential Vocabulary and Spelling Skills

I.)   *Reflect and Connect:* Complete the following sentences with words that are **familiar** to you and that make sense in each sentence. You may write more than one word choice for each blank space. **Do not** look at or study the new words yet. Answers will vary and your instructor will discuss them with you.

conservative   1. We saved money by being ___frugal___ in our spending.

considerable   2. There is a ___small___ amount of dirt on the floor that needs to be cleaned up.

conspicuous   3. There was a ___obvious___ show of wealth as each member of the family was given a new automobile.

constitute   4. What would ___be___ an ideal employment situation for you?

contemplate   5. I took time to ___decide___ on what the right decision was for me.

contemporary   6. She decorated the room in a ___lavish___ (modern) style.
contempt

7. The evil ruler showed great ___hatred___ towards his enemies.

contend   8. Are you willing to ___keep___ for that which is important to you?

contrary   9. ___Adverse___ to what you have heard, I do not live in a castle.
contrive

10. The two women tried to ___devise___ a plan that would keep them out of prison.

controversy 11. There is a ___debate___ over whether women should fight on the front lines in war.

conventional 12. A ___common___ mortgage is one that fits normal loan criteria.

converge   13. The two highways were designed to ___join___ at the center of town, which makes for good commerce.

copious   14. There was a ___plenty___ amount of food at the feast.
covert

15. The intelligence gathering community often engages in ___secret___ activities.

II.) ***Study the words and definitions below.*** These words and definitions are also on the enclosed CD Rom and may be printed out as study cards. The words are broken into letter groupings for easier spelling. Also, that is followed by a common definition, and common forms of the word that you might encounter. Your instructor will pronounce the words for you or you may want to use an audio dictionary for more help.

1. **conservative (con/ser/va/tive)** 1. Slower to change; content as is. 2. Preservative; having power to preserve in a safe or entire state, or from loss, waste or injury.
2. **considerable (con/sid/er/able)** 1. Important; valuable; or moderately large, according to the subject. 2. Worthy of consideration; worthy of regard or attention. 3. Respectable; deserving of notice; of some distinction.
3. **conspicuous (con/spic/u/ous)** Open to the view; obvious to the eye; easy to be seen; manifest.
4. **constitute (con/sti/tute)** 1. To set; to fix; to enact; to establish. 2. To form or compose; to give formal existence to; to make a thing what it is. 3. To appoint, depute or elect to an office or employment; to make and empower.
5. **contemplate (con/tem/plate)** 1. To view or consider with continued attention; to study; to meditate on; ponder. 2. To consider or have in view, in reference to a future act or event; to intend.
6. **contemporary (con/tem/por/ary)** 1. One who lives at the same time as another. 2. Modern.
7. **contempt (con/tem/pt)** 1. The act of despising; the act of viewing or considering and treating as mean, vile and worthless; disdain; hatred of what is mean or deemed vile. 2. The state of being despised; whence in a scriptural sense, shame, disgrace. 3. In law, disobedience of the rules and orders of a court which is a punishable offense.

8. **contend (con/tend)** 1. To strive, or to strive against; to struggle in opposition. 2. To strive; to use earnest efforts to obtain, or to defend and preserve. 3. To dispute earnestly; to strive in debate. 4. To reprove sharply; to chide; to strive to convince and reclaim. 5.To strive in opposition; to punish. 6. To quarrel; to dispute fiercely; to wrangle. The parties contend about trifles.

9. **contrary (con/tr/ary)** 1. Opposite; adverse; moving against or in an opposite direction; as contrary winds. 2. Opposite; contradictory; not merely different, but inconsistent or repugnant.

10. **contrive (con/tri/ve)** To invent; to devise; to plan; to scheme.

11. **controversy (con/tro/ver/sy)** 1. Dispute; debate; agitation of contrary opinions. 2. A suit in law; a case in which opposing parties contend for their respective claims before a tribunal. 3. Dispute; opposition carried on. 4. Opposition; resistance.

12. **conventional (con/ven/tion/al)** 1. Ordinary; common, average 2. Stipulated; formed by agreement.

13. **converge (con/ver/ge)** To tend to one point; to incline and approach nearer together, as two lines which continually approach each other.

14. **copious (co/pi/ous)** Abundant; plentiful; in great quantities; full; ample; furnishing full supplies.

15. **covert (co/vert)** 1. Covered; hid; private; secret; concealed. 2. Disguised. 3. Sheltered; not open or exposed. 4. Under cover, authority or protection.

III.) ***Match the words with their definitions.*** Draw a line from the word in the first column to the definition in the second column.

i. 1. conservative	a. a large amount
j. 2. considerable	b. to ponder
m. 3. conspicuous	c. modern
o. 4. constitute	d. to fight for
b. 5. contemplate	e. opposed to; opposite of
c. 6. contemporary	f. to scheme; to plan
n. 7. contempt	g. a disagreement
d. 8. contend	h. to come together; to merge
e. 9. contrary	i. slower to change
f. 10. contrive	j. more than enough
g. 11. controversy	k. ordinary
k. 12. conventional	l. secret; hidden
h. 13. converge	m. showy; out in the open
a. 14. copious	n. strong dislike
l. 15. covert	o. made up of

IV.) ***Puzzle work.*** Now try the interactive puzzle. Put the CD (that came with your workbook) into the computer, and work the puzzle. A paper copy of the puzzle is also included at the end of this chapter.

V.)   Write the correct new word in each sentence below:

conspicuous	constitute	contemplate	considerable	conservative
contend	contrary	contrive	contempt	contemporary
converge	copious	covert	conventional	controversy

1. We saved money by being _conservative_ in our spending.
2. There is a _considerable_ amount of dirt on the floor that needs to be cleaned up.
3. There was a(n) _conspicuous_ show of wealth as each member of the family was given a new automobile.
4. What would _constitute_ an ideal employment situation for you?
5. I took time to _contemplate_ on what the right decision was for me.
6. She decorated the room in a(n) _contemporary_ (modern) style.
7. The evil ruler showed great _contempt_ towards his enemies.
8. Are you willing to _contend_ for that which is important to you?
9. _Contrary_ to what you have heard, I do not live in a castle.
10. The two women tried to _contrive_ a plan that would keep them out of prison.
11. There is a(n) _controversy_ over whether women should fight on the front lines in war.
12. A(n) _conventional_ mortgage is one that fits normal loan criteria.
13. The two highways were designed to _converge_ at the center of town, which makes for good commerce.
14. There was a(n) _copious_ amount of food at the feast.
15. The intelligence gathering community often engages in _covert_ activities.

VI.)   Are you ready to take the practice test? You may take the practice test as many times as you want to. Simply insert the CD that came with book into your computer, go to "My Computer", open the CD by clicking on it, find the Practice test folder, choose this chapter's practice test and begin. (You will need a sheet of paper to write your answers on.) When finished, turn back to this chapter and correct your test. The answers are in the same order as exercise II.

VII.) Are you ready to use the words? Write a sentence for each word.

constitute	contemplate	conservative	conspicuous	considerable
contrary	contrive	contemporary	contend	contempt
copious	covert	controversy	converge	conventional

1. _____

2. _____

3. _____

4. _____

5. _____

6. _____

7. _____

8. _____

9. _____

10. _____

11. _____

12. _____

13. _____

14. _____

15. _____

VIII.) Your instructor may ask you to do the puzzle on the next page. It is the same as the one on your CD. You are able to do it here once or on the CD as many times as you'd like.

Across

1. showy; out in the open

6. to fight for

7. slower to change; more content as is

8. strong dislike

Down

1. more than enough

2. to come together; to merge

3. make up; form

4. to ponder

5. to scheme; to plan

6. secret; hidden

7. opposed to; opposite of

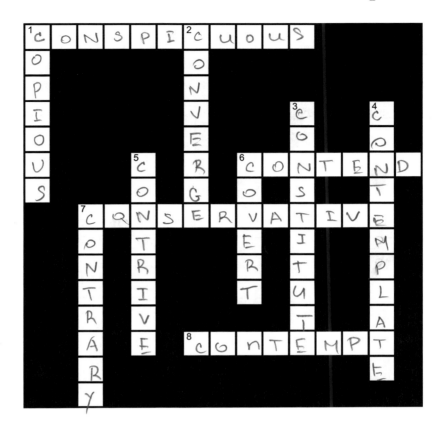

Rewrite your words

New word:		Practice writing the new word:		
Conservative				
Considerable				
Conspicuous				
Constitute				
Contemplate				
Contemporary				
Contempt				
contend				
contrary				
contrive				
controversy				
conventional				
converge				
copious				
covert				

Improving Essential Vocabulary and Spelling Skills

I.)   ***Reflect and Connect:*** Complete the following sentences with words that are familiar to you and that make sense in each sentence. You may write more than one word choice for each blank space. **Do not look at or study the new words yet.** Answers will vary and your instructor will discuss them with you.

commemorate **1.** To ___acknowledge___ the veterans, they set aside a day of remembrance called Memorial Day.

comparable **2.** The items sold at the *Designer Show Room* are ___equal___ in price to other designer stores.

compatible **3.** The young couple felt that they were very ___suitable___ and soon fell in love.

compel **4.** After much discussion, she was able to ___convince___ the prisoner to tell the truth.

compensate **5.** To ___make up___ for her feelings of inadequacy, she would overspend.

competent **6.** Joshua learned that with practice he could become a(n) ___better___ writer.

compile **7.** The lawyer was able to ___bring___ numerous documents and testimonies against the defendant.

complacent **8.** Some people become very ___lazy___ and they stop trying to better themselves.

composure **9.** The sergeant showed great ___attitude___ even in the midst of chaos.

comprehensive **10.** The test given to the eighth grade was meant to be a(n) ___general___ test that covered the subject matter for the whole year.

compromise **11.** Sometimes, even when we would rather not, we are forced to ___plan___ in order to move forward.

subjective **12.** When a person expresses their opinion on a topic, they are being ___successive___ rather than objective.

submissive **13.** A worker should be ___submissive___ to the will of the employer in all matters that are legal.

subsequent **14.** The result of ___consecutive___ questioning was a final breakthrough as the criminal finally confessed to his crimes.

subside **15.** The hurricane began to ___settle___ after five hours of unrelenting damage.

II.) ***Study the words and definitions below.*** These words and definitions are also on the enclosed CD Rom and may be printed out as study cards. The words are broken into letter groupings for easier spelling. Also, that is followed by a common definition, and common forms of the word that you might encounter. Your instructor will pronounce the words for you or you may want to use an audio dictionary for more help.

1. **commemorate (comm/em/or/ate)** To call to remembrance by a solemn act; to celebrate with honor and solemnity; to honor, as a person or event, by some act of respect or affection, intended to preserve the remembrance of that person or event.
2. **comparable (com/par/a/ble)** That may be compared; worthy of comparison; being of equal regard; that may be estimated as equal; Similar.
3. **compatible (com/pa/ti/ble)** Consistent; that may exist with; suitable; not incongruous; agreeable; able to get along.
4. **compel (com/pel)** 1. To drive or urge with force, or irresistibly; to constrain; to oblige; to necessitate, either by physical or moral force. 2. To drive together; to gather; to unite in a crowd or company.
5. **compensate (com/pen/sate)** 1. to counterbalance; to make amends for, to "make up for" feelings of inadequacy. 2. To give equal value to; to recompense; to give an equivalent for services, or an amount lost or bestowed; to return or bestow that which makes good a loss, or is estimated a sufficient recompense; 3. To be equivalent in value or effect.
6. **compile (com/pile)** 1. To put together; to build. 2. To write; to compose. 3. To collect parts or passages of books or writings into a book or pamphlet; to select and put together parts of an author, or to collect parts of different authors; or to collect and arrange separate papers, laws, or customs, in a book, code or system.

7. **composure (com/pos/ure)** 1. A settled state of the mind; sedateness; calmness; tranquility; not agitated. 2. The act of composing, or that which is composed; a composition. 3. The form, adjustment, or disposition of the various parts. 4. Frame; make; temperament. 5. Agreement; settlement of differences; composition. 6. The act of composing, or that which is composed; a composition.

8. **comprehensive (com/pre/hen/sive)** 1. Having the quality of comprising much, or including a great extent; extensive. 2. Having the power to comprehend or understand many things at once. 3. Complete.

9. **compromise (com/pro/mise)** 1. A mutual promise or contract of two parties in controversy, to refer their differences to the decision of arbitrators. 2. An amicable agreement between parties in controversy, to settle their differences by mutual concessions. 3. Mutual agreement; adjustment; to come to an agreement despite disagreement.

10. **subjective (sub/jec/tive)** Based on personal opinions; biased.

11. **submissive (sub/miss/ive)** 1. Yielding to the will or power of another; obedient. 2. Humble; acknowledging one's inferiority; testifying one's submission.

12. **subsequent (sub/se/qu/ent)** 1. Following in time; coming or being after something else at any time, indefinitely.
2. Following in the order of place or succession; succeeding.

13. **subside (sub/side)** 1. To fall into a state of quiet; to cease to rage; to be calmed; to become tranquil. 2. To tend downwards; to sink. 3. To abate; to be reduced. 4. To sink or fall to the bottom; to settle.

14. **competent (com/pe/tent)** 1. Suitable; fit; convenient; hence, sufficient, that is, fit for the purpose; adequate; skilled.
2. Qualified; fit; having legal capacity or power

15. **complacent (com/pla/cent)** Too much at ease.

III.) *Match the words with their definitions.* Draw a line from the word in the first column to the definition in the second column.

g. 1. commemorate

j. 2. comparable

h. 3. compatible

n. 4. compel

m. 5. compensate

l. 6. competent

i. 7. compile

d. 8. complacent

e. 9. composure

c. 10. comprehensive

o. 11. compromise

a. 12. subjective

f. 13. submissive

b. 14. subsequent

k. 15. subside

a. based on personal opinions

b. following in order

c. including all

d. too much at ease

e. not agitated

f. to submit to

g. to remember

h. able to get along

i. to put together

j. similar

k. to lessen

l. skilled

m. to pay for services

n. to urge to do; to force

o. to come to an agreement despite disagreement

IV.) *Puzzle work.* Now try the interactive puzzle. Put the CD (that came with your workbook) into the computer, and work the puzzle. A paper copy of the puzzle is also included at the end of this chapter.

V.)   Write the correct new word in each sentence below:

compatible	compensate	commemorate	compel	comparable
complacent	comprehensive	competent	composure	compile
submissive	subside	compromise	subsequent	subjective

1. To _commemorate_ the veterans, they set aside a day of remembrance called Memorial Day.

2. The items sold at the *Designer Show Room* are _comparable_ in price to other designer stores.

3. The young couple felt that they were very _compatible_ and soon fell in love.

4. After much discussion, she was able to _compel_ the prisoner to tell the truth.

5. To _compensate_ for her feelings of inadequacy, she would overspend.

6. Joshua learned that with practice he could become a(n) _competent_ writer.

7. The lawyer was able to _compile_ numerous documents and testimonies against the defendant.

8. Some people become very _complacement_ and they stop trying to better themselves.

9. The sergeant showed great _composure_ even in the midst of chaos.

10. The test given to the eighth grade was meant to be a _comprehensive_ test that covered the subject matter for the whole year.

11. Sometimes, even when we would rather not, we are forced to _compromise_ in order to move forward.

12. When a person expresses their opinion on a topic, they are being _subjective_ rather than objective.

13. A worker should be _submissive_ to the will of the employer in all matters that are legal.

14. The result of _subsequent_ questioning was a final breakthrough as the criminal confessed to his crimes.

15. The hurricane began to _subsuide_ after five hours of unrelenting damage.

VI.) Are you ready to take the practice test? You may take the practice test as many times as you want to. Simply insert the CD that came with book into your computer, go to "My Computer", open the CD by clicking on it, find the Practice test folder, choose this chapter's practice test and begin. (You will need a sheet of paper to write your answers on.) When finished, turn back to this chapter and correct your test. The answers are in the same order as exercise II.

VII.) Write a sentence for each word. Are you ready to use the words?

commemorate	comparable	compatible	compel	compensate
competent	compile	complacent	composure	comprehensive
compromise	subjective	submissive	subsequent	subside

1. _____
   _____

2. _____
   _____

3. _____
   _____

4. _____
   _____

5. _____
   _____

6. _____
   _____

7. _____
   _____

8. _____
   _____

9. _____
   _____

10. _____
   _____

11. _____
   _____

12. _____
   _____

13. _____
   _____

14. _____
   _____

15. _____
   _____

VIII.) Your instructor may ask you to do the puzzle on the next page. It is the same as the one on your CD. You are able to do it here once or on the CD as many times as you'd like.

Across

1. to submit to

4. not agitated

5. similar

7. too much at ease

8. including all

10. to put together

11. to pay for services or damages

Down

2. based on personal opinions

3. to remember

6. able to get along

7. skilled

8. to urge to do; to force

9. to lessen

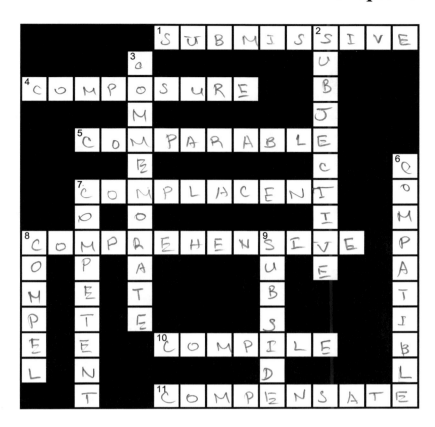

Rewrite your words

New word:		Practice writing the new word:		

Improving Essential Vocabulary and Spelling Skills

I.)   *Reflect and Connect:* Complete the following sentences with words that are **familiar** to you and that make sense in each sentence. You may write more than one word choice for each blank space. **Do not** look at or study the new words yet. Answers will vary and your instructor will discuss them with you.

encroach

endeavor

endorse

enigma

immaculate

immutable

impartial

impasse

impassive

implausible

implication

implicite

implore

improvise

impulsive

1. A person should not ____trespass____ on another's property without permission.
2. We should all ____strive____ to become useful members of society.
3. Companies often use movie stars to __advertise__ their product.
4. The events surrounding the Kennedy assassination have remained a(n) ____secret____ to this day.
5. Navy officers expect their sailors to keep a(n) ____clean____ ship.
6. The representatives were ____stable____ in their position on tax increases; they were not going to raise taxes in an election year.
7. The judge was very __consistent__ in her judgments; all defendants were given fair trials.
8. The legislature came to a(n) __conclusion__ and were unable to pass a budget.
9. Scott's face showed a(n) __reserved__ attitude; there was no show of emotion.
10. The defendant's alibis seemed very ____false____ and unlikely to sway a jury in his direction.
11. The __situation__ was clear; it would be difficult to defend someone who had such contrived alibis.
12. Contained in his testimony was the __practical__ desire to fool the judge and jury.
13. "I ____ask____ you to consider all of the evidence before you make your final decision," the defense lawyer shouted to the jury.
14. On stage, actors often have to __devise__ until they can remember their lines.
15. Karen is a(n) __careless__ shopper who spends hundreds of dollars on clothes, even when it is not necessary.

II.) *Study the words and definitions below.* These words and definitions are also on the enclosed CD Rom and may be printed out as study cards. The words are broken into letter groupings for easier spelling. Also, that is followed by a common definition, and common forms of the word that you might encounter. Your instructor will pronounce the words for you or you may want to use an audio dictionary for more help.

1. **encroach (en/cr/oach)** 1. To enter on the rights and possession of another; to intrude; to take possession of what belongs to another, by gradual advances into his limits or jurisdiction, and usurping a part of his rights. 2. To creep on gradually without right. 3. To pass the proper bounds, and enter on another's rights.
2. **endeavor (en/dea/vor)** An effort; an essay; an attempt; an exertion of physical strength, or the intellectual powers, towards the attainment of an object.
3. **endorse (en/dor/se)** 1. To support. 2. To write on the back of a paper or written instrument.
4. **enigma (en/ig/ma)** 1. A mystery. 2. A dark saying, in which some known thing is concealed under obscure language; an obscure question; a riddle. A question, saying or painting, containing a hidden meaning, which is proposed to be guessed.
5. **immaculate (imm/a/cu/late)** 1. Spotless; pure; unstained; undefiled; without blemish; perfectly clean.
6. **immutable (imm/u/ta/ble)** Invariable; unalterable; not capable of change.
7. **impartial (im/par/tial)** 1. Not partial; not biased in favor of one party more than another; indifferent; unprejudiced; disinterested. 2. Not favoring one party more than another; equitable; just; fair; unbiased.
8. **impasse (im/passe)** 1. No way out. 2. Not able to pass
9. **impassive (im/pass/ive)** 1. Not susceptible of pain or suffering. 2. unemotional

10. implausible (im/plaus/ible) Not wearing the appearance of truth or credibility, and not likely to be believed.

11. implication (im/pli/ca/tion) 1. Suggestion. 2. An implying, or that which is implied, but not expressed; a tacit inference, or something fairly to be understood, though not expressed in words.

12. implicit (im/pli/cit) 1. Entangled; an essential part of. 2. Implied. 3. Resting on another; trusting to the word or authority of another, without doubting or reserve, or without examining into the truth of the thing itself.

13. implore (im/pl/ore) 1. To call upon or for, in supplication; to beseech; to pray earnestly; to petition with urgency; to entreat. 2. To ask earnestly; to beg.

14. improvise (im/pro/vise) To create without much planning

15. impulsive (im/pul/sive) Acting with little thought of the consequences.

III.) *Match the words with their definitions.* Draw a line from the word in the first column to the definition in the second column.

f. 1. encroach
c. 2. endeavor
j. 3. endorse
l. 4. enigma
k. 5. immaculate
m. 6. immutable
e. 7. impartial
b. 8. impasse
o. 9. impassive
n. 10. implausible
h. 11. implication
g. 12. implicit
a. 13. implore
d. 14. improvise
i. 15. impulsive

a. to beg
b. no way out
c. to put forth much effort
d. to create with little planning
e. fair; unbiased
f. to trespass; to be uninvited
g. an essential part of
h. a suggestion
i. little thought of consequences
j. to support
k. perfectly clean
l. mystery
m. not changeable
n. not likely; not very believable
o. unemotional

IV.) *Puzzle work.* Now try the interactive puzzle. Put the CD (that came with your workbook) into the computer, and work the puzzle. A paper copy of the puzzle is also included at the end of this chapter.

endeavor	endorse	immaculate	encroach	enigma
impartial	impasse	implausible	immutable	impassive
implicit	implore	impulsive	implication	improvise

V.) **Write the correct new word in each sentence below:**

1. A person should not __encroach__ on another's property without permission.

2. We should all __endeavor__ to become useful members of society.

3. Companies often use movie stars to __endorse__ their product.

4. The events surrounding the Kennedy assassination have remained a(n) __enigma__ to this day.

5. Navy officers expect their sailors to keep a(n) __immaculate__ ship.

6. The representatives were __immutable__ in their position on tax increases; they were not going to raise taxes in an election year.

7. The judge was very __impartial__ in her judgments; all defendants were given fair trials.

8. The legislature came to a(n) __impasse__ and were unable to pass a budget.

9. Scott's face showed a(n) __impassive__ attitude; there was no show of emotion.

10. The defendant's alibis seemed very __implausible__ and unlikely to sway a jury in his direction.

11. The __implication__ was clear; it would be difficult to defend someone who had such contrived alibis.

12. Contained in his testimony was the __implicit__ desire to fool the judge and jury.

13. "I __implore__ you to consider all of the evidence before you make your final decision," the defense lawyer shouted to the jury.

14. On stage, actors often have to __improvise__ until they can remember their lines.

15. Karen is a(n) __impulsive__ shopper who spends hundreds of dollars on clothes, even when it is not necessary.

VI.) **Are you ready to take the practice test?** You may take the practice test as many times as you want to. Simply insert the CD that came with book into your computer, go to "My Computer", open the CD by clicking on it, find the Practice test folder, choose this chapter's practice test and begin. (You will need a sheet of paper to write your answers on.) When finished, turn back to this chapter and correct your test. The answers are in the same order as exercise II.

VII.) Are you ready to use the words? Write a sentence for each word.

endeavor	endorse	immaculate	encroach	enigma
impartial	impasse	implausible	immutable	impassive
implicit	implore	impulsive	implication	improvise

1. _____

2. _____

3. _____

4. _____

5. _____

6. _____

7. _____

8. _____

9. _____

10. _____

11. _____

12. _____

13. _____

14. _____

15. _____

VIII.) Your instructor may ask you to do the puzzle on the next page. It is the same as the one on your CD. You are able to do it here once or on the CD as many times as you'd like.

Across

1. to create without much planning

4. mystery

7. not changeable

8. little thought of consequences

11. perfectly clean

12. to put forth much effort

Down

1. fair; unbiased

2. an essential part of

3. not likely; not very believable

5. a suggestion

6. unemotional

9. no way out

10. to beg

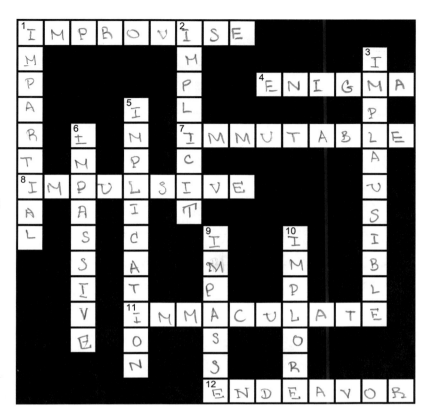

Rewrite your words

New word:		Practice writing the new word:		
Encroach				
Endeavor				
Endorse				
Enigma				
Immaculate				
Immutable				
Impartial				
Impasse				
Impassive				
Implausible				
Implication				
Implicit				
Implore				
Improvise				
Impulsive				

Improving Essential Vocabulary and Spelling Skills

I.)   *Reflect and Connect:* Complete the following sentences with words that are **familiar** to you and that make sense in each sentence. You may write more than one word choice for each blank space. **Do not look at or study the new words yet.** Answers will vary and your instructor will discuss them with you.

exemplary
exhaustive
1. Mike is a(n) __excellent__ student and receives straight A's in school.
2. The President asked for a(n) __thorough__ plan that would cover all possible outcomes.

expedient
3. In an emergency, it is __wise__ to call 911.

explicit
4. The conduct of the demonstrators was very __explanitory__ and left no questions as to their objectives.

extol
5. Religious leaders often __praise__ virtues that they hope their members will adopt.

extraneous
6. Some of his __daily__ activities outside of work are golfing and fishing.

extortion
7. The organized crime figures used __blackmailing__ as a means to support their lavish lifestyles.

exuberance
8. He showed a great deal of __respect__ when he received his new position.

exemplify
9. The scene on the bow of the Titanic seemed to __demonstrate__ the lovers' momentary joy.

transcend
10. The new employee was able to __excel__ all expectations.

transitory
11. The tornado was very __suttle__ since it lasted only a very short time.

transgression
12. Richard's bad conduct was a serious __violation__ of the law.

transpire
13. After the hurricane, the residents wondered what would __happen__ next.

tranquility
14. Visitors to Hawaii enjoy a lot of __rest__.

transmission
15. Scientists wondered about the __absense__ of the AIDS virus and began to search for ways of preventing its spread.

II.) ***Study the words and definitions below.*** These words and definitions are also on the enclosed CD Rom and may be printed out as study cards. The words are broken into letter groupings for easier spelling. Also, that is followed by a common definition, and common forms of the word that you might encounter. Your instructor will pronounce the words for you or you may want to use an audio dictionary for more help.

1. **exemplary (ex/em/pl/ary)** 1. Serving for a pattern or model for imitation; worthy of imitation. 2. Illustrating; representing well.
2. **exhaustive (ex/haus/tive)** Very complete; total; entire.
3. **expedient (ex/ped/ient)** 1. Useful; profitable. 2. Quick; expeditious; convenient. 3. Literally, hastening; urging forward. Hence, tending to promote the object proposed; fit or suitable for the purpose; proper under the circumstances.
4. **explicit (ex/pli/cit) 2.** Plain; open; clear; unreserved; having no disguised meaning or reservation; clearly expressed.
5. **extol (ex/tol)** To raise in words or eulogy; to praise; to exalt in commendation; to magnify; to put forth, to encourage.
6. **extraneous (ex/tran/e/ous)** Foreign; not belonging to a thing; existing without; not intrinsic; extra.
7. **extortion (ex/tor/tion)** 1. The act of extorting; the act or practice of wresting any thing from a person by force, duress, menaces, authority, or by any undue exercise of power; illegal exaction; illegal compulsion to pay money, or to do some other act. 2. Force or illegal compulsion by which any thing is taken from a person. 3. To require money by force.
8. **exuberance (ex/u/ber/ance)** 1. An abundance; an overflowing quantity; richness. 2. Enthusiasm.
9. **exemplify (ex/em/pli/fy)** To show or illustrate by example.
10. **transcend (trans/cend)** 1. To rise above; to surmount. 2. To pass over; to go beyond. 3. To surpass; to outgo; to excel; to exceed.

11. **transpire (trans/pire)** 1. To happen or come to pass; to take place. 2. To escape from secrecy; to become public. 3. To be emitted through the pores of the skin; to exhale.

12. **transgression (trans/gress/ion)** 1. The act of passing over or beyond any law or rule of moral duty; the violation of a law or known principle of rectitude; breach of command; violation of law, disobedience, rebellion. 2. Fault; offense; crime.

13. **transmission (trans/miss/ion) 1.** Passing on of something. 2. The passing of a substance through a body as of light through a glass. 3. The act of sending from one place or person to another.

14. **transitory (trans/i/tory)** Passing without continuance; continuing a short time; fleeting; speedily vanishing.

15. **tranquility (tran/quil/ity)** Quiet; calm; undisturbed; peaceful; not agitated.

III.) *Match the words with their definitions.* Draw a line from the word in the first column to the definition in the second column.

o. 1. exemplary   a. peaceful
l. 2. exhaustive   b. violation of the law
m. 3. expedient   c. to put forth; to encourage
n. 4. explicit   d. extra
c. 5. extol   e. enthusiasm
d. 6. extraneous   f. to represent well
g. 7. extortion   g. to require money by force
e. 8. exuberance   h. to go beyond
f. 9. exemplify   i. passing on of something
h. 10. transcend   j. to pass quickly
k. 11. transpire   k. to take place
b. 12. transgression   l. very complete
i. 13. transmission   m. convenient
j. 14. transitory   n. clearly expressed
a. 15. tranquility   o. to serve as an example

IV.) *Puzzle work.* Now try the interactive puzzle. Put the CD (that came with your workbook) into the computer, and work the puzzle. A paper copy of the puzzle is also included at the end of this chapter.

V.)   **Write the correct new word in each sentence below:**

expedient	extol	exemplary	exhaustive	explicit
exuberance	transcend	extraneous	extortion	exemplify
transmission	tranquility	transitory	transgression	transpire

1. Mike is a(n) _exemplary_ student and receives straight A's in high school.
2. The President asked for a(n) _exhaustive_ plan that would cover all possible outcomes.
3. In an emergency, it is _expedient_ to call 911.
4. The conduct of the demonstrators was very _explicit_ and left no questions as to their objectives.
5. Religious leaders often _extol_ virtues that they hope their members will adopt.
6. Some of his _extraneous_ activities outside of work are golfing and fishing.
7. The organized crime figures used _extortion_ as a means to support their lavish lifestyles.
8. He showed a great deal of _exuberance_ when he received his new position.
9. The scene on the bow of the Titanic seemed to _exemplify_ the lovers' momentary joy.
10. The new employee was able to _transcend_ all expectations.
11. The tornado was very _transpire_ since it lasted only a very short time.
12. Richard's bad conduct was a serious _transgression_ of the law.
13. After the hurricane, the residents wondered what would _transmission_ next.
14. Visitors to Hawaii enjoy a lot of _transitory_ .
15. Scientists wondered about the _tranquility_ of the AIDS virus and began to search for ways of preventing its spread.

VI.) Are you ready to take the practice test? You may take the practice test as many times as you want to. Simply insert the CD that came with book into your computer, go to "My Computer", open the CD by clicking on it, find the Practice test folder, choose this chapter's practice test and begin. (You will need a sheet of paper to write your answers on.) When finished, turn back to this chapter and correct your test. The answers are in the same order as exercise II.

VII.) Write a sentence for each new word. Are you ready to use the new words? Write a sentence for each new word.

expedient	extol	exhaustive	explicit	exemplary
exuberance	transcend	extortion	exemplify	extraneous
transmission	tranquility	transgression	transitory	transpire

1. _____
2. _____
3. _____
4. _____
5. _____
6. _____
7. _____
8. _____
9. _____
10. _____
11. _____
12. _____
13. _____
14. _____
15. _____

VIII.) Your instructor may ask you to do the puzzle on the next page. It is the same as the one on your CD. You are able to do it here once or on the CD as many times as you'd like.

Across

2. to require money by force

4. extra

7. to pass quickly

8. passing on of something

10. to put forth; to encourage

11. to serve as an example

12. violation of the law

Down

1. very complete

3. to take place

5. to go beyond

6. to represent well

7. peaceful

9. clearly expressed

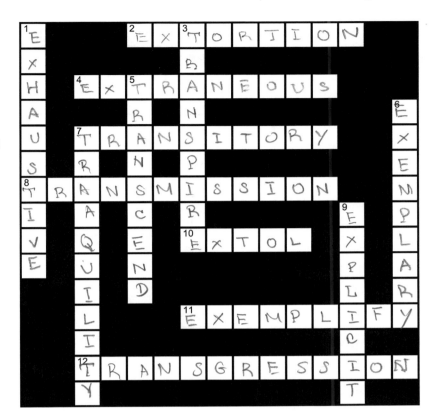

Rewrite your words

New word:		Practice writing the new word:		

Improving Essential Vocabulary and Spelling Skills

I.) *Reflect and Connect:* Complete the following sentences with words that are **familiar** to you and that make sense in each sentence. You may write more than one word choice for each blank space. **Do not** look at or study the new words yet. Answers will vary and your instructor will discuss them with you.

recede 1. Most men hate it when their hair begins to __fall off__.

recession 2. As the stock market slipped, some analysts declared that we were in a __recession__.

recipient 3. Many of the people who live in that apartment building are __beneficiary__ of welfare.

reciprocate 4. Mary's neighbors had shown kindness to her during her illness, so Mary wanted to __return favor__ by hosting a party in their honor.

reconcile 5. Bill wanted to __settle__ with Hillary because of the wrongs he had committed, so he begged for her forgiveness.

rectify 6. Germany sought for ways to __fix__ the evil deeds that occurred during World War II.

recur 7. In "Tornado Alley," tornadoes are likely to __reappear__ since they have often occurred in the past.

redundant 8. It's __unecessary__ to say, "The meeting has been postponed until later" since postponed means put off until a later time.

refrain 9. Two men were in an argument and they both tried hard to __obtain__ from any physical contact.

refute 10. Lawyers have to __disprove__ many accusations.

rehabilitate 11. Joe had to __recover__ from his alcohol problem.

reprisal 12. The citizens were not willing to forgive, and therefore wanted __avenge__ for the harm that they suffered.

renounce 13. Most people __reject__ evil deeds, and instead strive to do that which is good.

revoke 14. The DMV will __confiscate__ a driver's license for drug or alcohol related accidents.

revert 15. Manuel will probably __return__ back to his old eating habits and gain back the weight he lost.

II.) *Study the words and definitions below.* These words and definitions are also on the enclosed CD Rom and may be printed out as study cards. The words are broken into letter groupings for easier spelling. Also, that is followed by a common definition, and common forms of the word that you might encounter. Your instructor will pronounce the words for you or you may want to use an audio dictionary for more help.

1. **recede (re/cede)** 1. To go back; move in a backward direction; to retreat; to withdraw.
2. **recession (re/cess/ion)** 1. A state of economic decline. 2. The act of withdrawing, retiring or retreating. 3. The act of receding from a claim, or of relaxing a demand.
3. **recipient (re/ci/pient)** One who receives something.
4. **reciprocate (re/ci/pro/cate)** To exchange; to interchange; to give and return mutually; to give in return for something previously received.
5. **reconcile (re/con/cile)** 1. To make amends; to re-establish a close relationship. 2. To conciliate anew; to call back into union and friendship the affections which have been alienated; to restore to friendship or favor after estrangement. 3. To adjust; to settle.
6. **rectify (rec/ti/fy)** 1. To make right; to correct that which is wrong, erroneous or false; to amend.
7. **recur (re/cur)** To occur again.
8. **redundant (re/dun/dant)** Needlessly repetitive; not necessary to say because its meaning is already clear; using more words or images than are necessary or useful.
9. **refrain (re/fr/ain)** To hold back; to restrain; to keep from action.
10. **refute (re/fute)** To disprove and overthrow by argument, evidence or countervailing proof; to prove to be false or erroneous.

11. **rehabilitate (re/ha/bil/i/tate)** 1. To restore to a healthier condition. 2. To restore to a former capacity; to reinstate; to qualify again.

12. **reprisal (re/pri/sal)** 1. The seizure or taking of any thing from an enemy by way of retaliation or indemnification for something taken or detained by him. 2. the result of revenge; retaliation.

13. **renounce (re/noun/ce)** 1. To disown; to disclaim; to reject; as a title or claim; to refuse to own or acknowledge as belonging to. 2. To deny; to cast off; to reject; to disclaim. 3. To cast off or reject, as a connection or possession; to forsake.

14. **revoke (re/voke)** 1. To recall; to repeal; to reverse; to take away. 3. To draw back.

15. **revert (re/vert)** 1. To turn back; to turn to the contrary; to reverse; to go back to a previous condition.

III.) *Match the words with their definitions.* Draw a line from the word in the first column to the definition in the second column.

m.1. recede   **a. to take away**
g. 2. recession   **b. to occur again**
f. 3. recipient   **c. needlessly repetitive**
l. 4. reciprocate   **d. to reject**
j. 5. reconcile   **e. to correct**
e. 6. rectify   **f. one who receives**
b. 7. recur   **g. economic decline**
c. 8. redundant   **h. to disagree**
k. 9. refrain   **i. to restore to health**
h.10. refute   **j. to make amends**
i.11. rehabilitate   **k. to hold back**
n.12. reprisal   **l. mutual exchange**
d.13. renounce   **m. to move backward**
a.14. revoke   **n. revenge**
o.15. revert   **o. to go back to a previous condition**

IV.) *Puzzle work.* Now try the interactive puzzle. Put the CD (that came with your workbook) into the computer, and work the puzzle. A paper copy of the puzzle is also included at the end of this chapter.

V.) Write the correct new word in each sentence below:

recession	recipient	reconcile	recede	reciprocate
recur	redundant	refute	rectify	refrain
reprisal	renounce	revert	rehabilitate	revoke

1. Most men hate it when their hair begins to __recede__ .
2. As the stock market slipped, some analysts declared that we were in a __recession__ .
3. Many of the people who live in that apartment building are __recipient__ of welfare.
4. Mary's neighbors had shown kindness to her during her illness, so Mary wanted to __reciprocate__ by hosting a party in their honor.
5. Bill wanted to __reconcile__ with Hillary because of the wrongs he had committed, so he begged for her forgiveness.
6. Germany sought for ways to __rectify__ the evil deeds that occurred during World War II.
7. In "Tornado Alley," tornadoes are likely to __recur__ since they have often occurred in the past.
8. It's __redundant__ to say, "The meeting has been postponed until later" since postponed means put off until a later time.
9. Two men were in an argument and they both tried hard to __refrain__ from any physical contact.
10. Lawyers have to __refute__ many accusations.
11. Joe had to __rehabilitate__ from his alcohol problem.
12. The citizens were not willing to forgive and therefore wanted __reprisal__ for the harm that they suffered.
13. Most people __renounce__ evil deeds and instead strive to do that which is good.
14. The DMV will __revoke__ a driver's license for drug or alcohol related accidents.
15. Manuel will probably __revert__ back to his old eating habits and gain back the weight he lost.

VI.) Are you ready to take the practice test? You may take the practice test as many times as you want to. Simply insert the CD that came with book into your computer, go to "My Computer", open the CD by clicking on it, find the Practice test folder, choose this chapter's practice test and begin. (You will need a sheet of paper to write your answers on.) When finished, turn back to this chapter and correct your test. The answers are in the same order as exercise II.

VI.) **Are you ready to use the words?** Write a sentence for each word.

recipient	reconcile	recede	recession	reciprocate
redundant	refute	rectify	recur	refrain
renounce	revert	rehabilitate	reprisal	revoke

1. _____

2. _____

3. _____

4. _____

5. _____

6. _____

7. _____

8. _____

9. _____

10. _____

11. _____

12. _____

13. _____

14. _____

15. _____

VIII.) **Your instructor may ask you to do the puzzle on the next page. It is the same as the one on your CD. You are able to do it here once or on the CD as many times as you'd like.**

Across

1. needlessly repetitive

2. a state of economic decline

3. to occur again

5. to go back to a previous condition

7. to disagree and to give the reasons

10. to give up; to reject

11. to restore to a healthier condition

Down

1. to correct after a wrong has been committed

2. the result of revenge

3. to take away

4. mutual exchange

6. one who receives something

8. To make amends

9. to go back

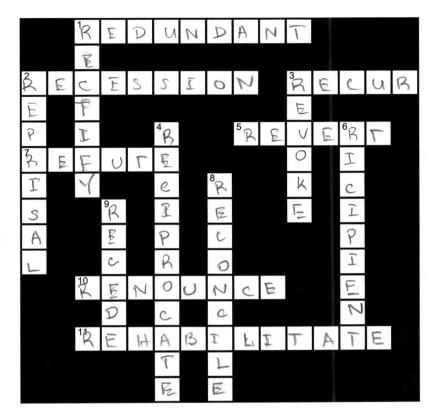

Rewrite your words

New word:		Practice writing the new word:		
recede				
recession				
recipient				
reciprocate				
reconcile				
rectify				
recur				
redundant				
refrain				
refute				
rehabilitate				
reprisal				
renounce				
revoke				
revert				

Improving Essential Vocabulary and Spelling Skills

I.) **Reflect and Connect:** Complete the following sentences with words that are **familiar** to you and that make sense in each sentence. You may write more than one word choice for each blank space. **Do not** look at or study the new words yet. Answers will vary and your instructor will discuss them with you.

repressive 1. The government of Iraq was a very ___subduing___ government which treated its people unjustly.

rescind 2. The government decided to ___cancel___ its offer of protection when they found out that the spy was a double agent.

retort 3. The DMV agent was quick to ___reply___, "You'll have to wait until your number is called!"

retract 4. The politician had to ___draw back___ his earlier statement once he was proven wrong.

revulsion 5. There was a feeling of ___rejection___ when they learned how Lacey had died.

revitalize 6 A swim in the pool may ___renew___ you after a long hot day at work.

reminisce 7 The two old friends liked to ___think___ about old times.

relevant 8. The judge threw out the weak testimony and declared that it was not ___connected___ to the case.

remorse 9. He showed no ___guilt___ for the crime he committed.

repertoire 10. The top model had a large ___amount___ of experience.

reprimand 11. It is the place of the parents to ___discipline___ their children if they do not behave.

resolution 12. The founders of our country had a firm ___beliefs___ to gain freedom.

relentless 13. The ___severe___ battle seemed like it would never end.

renown 14. After winning an Academy Award, an actor is considered to be one of great ___fame___.

render 15. David tried to ___accommodate___ help to the accident victims until the ambulance arrived.

II.) *Study the words and definitions below.* These words and definitions are also on the enclosed CD Rom and may be printed out as study cards. The words are broken into letter groupings for easier spelling. Also, that is followed by a common definition, and common forms of the word that you might encounter. Your instructor will pronounce the words for you or you may want to use an audio dictionary for more help.

1. **repressive (re/pre/ss/ive)** 1. Having power to crush; tending to subdue or restrain. 2. Suppressive; restraining; inhibiting.
2. **rescind (res/cind)** To abrogate; to revoke; to annul; to vacate an act by the enacting authority or by superior authority.
3. **retort (re/tort)** 1. To make a severe reply. 2. To throw back; to reverberate. 3. To return an argument, accusation, censure or incivility.
4. **retract (re/tr/act)** 1. To take back; to rescind. 2. To recall, as a declaration, words or saying; to disavow; to recant.
5. **revulsion (re/vul/sion)** Disgust; The act of holding or drawing back.
6. **revitalize (re/vi/tal/ize)** 1. To restore to a healthy condition; 2. Refresh.
7. **reminisce (re/min/isce)** To fondly think back on earlier times
8. **relevant (rel/e/vant)** Pertinent; applicable; relating to; pertaining to; a part of.
9. **remorse (re/mor/se)** 1. The keen pain or anguish excited by a sense of guilt; compunction of conscience for a crime committed. 2. Sympathetic sorrow; pity; compassion.
10. **repertoire (re/per/toire)** The accumulation of songs, plays, poems, etc that a person has ready to perform.

11. reprimand (re/pri/mand) 1. To reprove severely; to correct; rebuke; admonish. 2. To reprove publicly and officially, in execution of a sentence.

12. resolution (res/o/lu/tion) 1. Fixed purpose or determination of mind. 2. The act or process of unraveling or disentangling perplexities. 3. The effect of fixed purpose; firmness, steadiness or constancy in execution, implying courage.

13. relentless (re/lent/less) With very little relief; ongoing; without stopping.

14. renown (re/nown) 1. Fame; celebrity; exalted reputation derived from the extensive praise of great achievements or accomplishments.

15. render (ren/der) To give on demand; to give; to submit.

III.) ***Match the words with their definitions.*** Draw a line from the word in the first column to the definition in the second column.

g. 1. repressive   a. a feeling of guilt
f. 2. rescind   b. to submit
e. 3. retort   c. determination
i. 4. retract   d. accumulation of talents
n. 5. revulsion   e. sharp quick reply
m. 6. revitalize   f. make void
k. 7. reminisce   g. inhibiting
h. 8. relevant   h. relating to
a. 9. remorse   i. to take back
d. 10. repertoire   j. well known
l. 11. reprimand   k. think fondly back on
c. 12. resolution   l. to rebuke
o. 13. relentless   m. restore to health
j. 14. renown   n. disgust
b. 15. render   o. with very little relief

IV.) ***Puzzle work.*** Now try the interactive puzzle. Put the CD (that came with your workbook) into the computer, and work the puzzle. A paper copy of the puzzle is also included at the end of this chapter.

V.)   Write the correct new word in each sentence below:

rescind	retract	revulsion	repressive	retort
reminisce	remorse	repertoire	revitalize	relevant
resolution	renown	render	reprimand	relentless

1. The government of Iraq was a very _repressive_ government which treated its people unjustly.

2. The government decided to _rescind_ its offer of protection when they found out that the spy was a double agent.

3. The DMV agent was quick to _retort_, "You'll have to wait until your number is called!"

4. The politician had to _retract_ his earlier statement once he was proven wrong.

5. There was a feeling of _revulsion_ when they learned how Lacey had died.

6. A swim in the pool may _revitalize_ you after a long hot day at work.

7. The two old friends liked to _reminisce_ about old times.

8. The judge threw out the weak testimony and declared that it was not _relevant_ to the case.

9. He showed no _remorse_ for the crime he committed.

10. The top model had a large _repertoire_ of experience.

11. It is the place of the parents to _reprimand_ their children if they do not behave.

12. The founders of our country had a firm _resolution_ to gain freedom.

13. The _relentless_ battle seemed like it would never end.

14. After winning an Academy Award, an actor is considered to be one of great _renown_.

15. David tried to _render_ help to the accident victims until the ambulance arrived.

VI.) Are you ready to take the practice test? You may take the practice test as many times as you want to. Simply insert the CD that came with book into your computer, go to "My Computer", open the CD by clicking on it, find the Practice test folder, choose this chapter's practice test and begin. (You will need a sheet of paper to write your answers on.) When finished, turn back to this chapter and correct your test. The answers are in the same order as exercise II.

VII.) Are you ready to use the words? Write a sentence for each word.

rescind	retract	repressive	revulsion	retort
reminisce	remorse	revitalize	repertoire	relevant
resolution	renown	reprimand	render	relentless

1. _____

2. _____

3. _____

4. _____

5. _____

6. _____

7. _____

8. _____

9. _____

10. _____

11. _____

12. _____

13. _____

14. _____

15. _____

VIII.) Your instructor may ask you to do the puzzle on the next page. It is the same as the one on your CD. You are able to do it here once or on the CD as many times as you'd like.

Across

1. to take back

4. a feeling of guilt; sorrow

6. with very little relief; ongoing; without stopping

9. suppressive; restraining; inhibiting

11. determination; decisiveness

12. to give; to submit

Down

1. to correct; rebuke; admonish

2. relating to; pertaining to; a part of

3. to restore to a healthy condition

4. make void; repeal; annul

5. well known; honored; acclaimed

7. disgust

8. the accumulation of songs, plays, poems, etc

10. a sharp quick reply

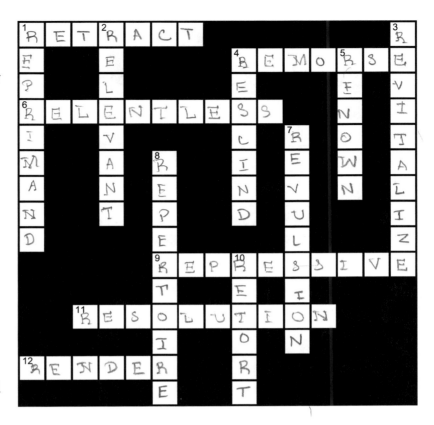

Rewrite your words

New word:	Practice writing the new word:		

Improving Essential Vocabulary and Spelling Skills

I.) **Reflect and Connect:** Complete the following sentences with words that are **familiar** to you and that make sense in each sentence. You may write more than one word choice for each blank space. **Do not look at or study the new words yet.** Answers will vary and your instructor will discuss them with you.

incentive **1.** There is a ten-dollar ___reward___ if you finish your work early.

incessant **2.** The ___constant___ arguing in Congress left everyone exhausted.

incidental **3.** Tony's contribution to the project was very ___minor___ since he rarely contributed anything to the group effort.

incisive **4.** Monica's ideas were very ___profound___ and quickly adopted by the committee.

inclination **5.** My first ___thought___, when I hear someone choking, is to hit him or her on the back.

incorporate **6.** The seamstress tried to ___add___ diamonds on the dress as part of the design.

indict **7.** The Grand Jury was ready to ___sentence___ her for the crime.

indigent **8.** His inability to find work reduced him to the status of a(n) ___impoverish___.

induce **9.** The doctors wanted to ___persuade___ labor for Mrs. Hill because her due date had passed.

indulgent **10.** The two gamblers lived a(n) ___lavish___ life in Las Vegas.

infringe **11.** Standing too close to another person tends to ___encroach___ on their "space."

infuriate **12.** The uncaring politician's attitude towards the public tended to ___insult___ many people.

initiate **13.** I'm so shy; I depend on others to ___start___ friendships.

innovation **14.** The plasma television is a wonderful ___improvement___.

integrity **15.** Wanda showed ___honesty___ when she came forth to tell the truth.

II.) *Study the words and definitions below.* These words and definitions are also on the enclosed CD Rom and may be printed out as study cards. The words are broken into letter groupings for easier spelling. Also, that is followed by a common definition, and common forms of the word that you might encounter. Your instructor will pronounce the words for you or you may want to use an audio dictionary for more help.

1. **incentive (in/cen/tive)** 1. That which moves the mind or operates on the passions; that which incites or has a tendency to incite to determination or action; that which prompts to good or ill; encouragement; something that produces a desire to move toward a desired end; 2. Bonus, reward

2. **incessant (in/cess/ant)** Unceasing; uninterrupted; continual; unrelenting.

3. **incidental (in/ci/den/tal)** 1. minor; subordinate; casual; 2. Unimportant, insignificant.

4. **incisive (in/cis/ive)** 1. Having the quality of cutting or separating the superficial part of any thing. 2. penetrating; sharp; clear.

5. **inclination (in/clin/a/tion)** 1. A leaning; any deviation of a body or line from an upright position, or from a parallel line, towards another body. 2. A leaning of the mind or will; a disposition more favorable to one thing than to another; a tendency. 3. Love; affection; regard; desire; with for. 4. Disposition of mind.

6. **incorporate (in/cor/por/ate)** To unite so as to make a part of another body; to be mixed or blended; to grow into ; to unite into one.

7. **indict (in/dict)** In law, to accuse or charge with a crime or misdemeanor, in writing, by a grand jury under oath.

8. **indigent (in/di/gent)** Destitute of property or means of comfortable subsistence; needy; poor; an impoverished person; beggar.

9. **induce (in/duce)** 1. To produce; to bring on; to cause. 2. To lead, as by persuasion or argument; to prevail on; to incite; to influence by motives.

10. **indulgent (in/dul/gent)** 1. Yielding to the wishes, desires, or appetites of those under one's care; 2. compliant; not opposing or restraining; 3. lenient; easygoing; liberal; 4. lavish.

11. **infringe (in/fr/inge)** To break; to violate; to transgress; to go beyond the proper limits.

12. **infuriate (in/fur/i/ate)** To make furious or mad; to enrage; to make very angry.

13. **initiate (in/i/tia/te)** 1. To begin. 2. To introduce into a new state or society.

14. **innovation (inn/o/va/tion)** 1. Change made by the introduction of something new; change in established laws, customs, rites or practices. 2. Something newly created, an invention.

15. **integrity (in/te/gri/ty)** 1. Purity; genuine, unadulterated, unimpaired state; possessing morals; having principles; honoring your commitments. 2. Wholeness; entireness; unbroken state. 3. The entire, unimpaired state of any thing, particularly of the mind; moral soundness or purity; incorruptness; uprightness; honesty.

incidental	inclination	incentive	incessant	incisive
indigent	indulgent	incorporate	indict	induce
initiate	integrity	infringe	infuriate	innovation

III.) ***Match the words with their definitions.*** Draw a line from the word in the first column to the definition in the second column.

a. 1. incentive
k. 2. incessant
e. 3. incidental
l. 4. incisive
o. 5. inclination
d. 6. incorporate
n. 7. infringe
i. 8. indict
f. 9. infuriate
m. 10. indigent
a. 11. initiate
b. 12. induce
c. 13. innovation
h. 14. indulgent
j. 15. integrity

a. to begin
b. to bring about
c. something newly created
d. to combine
e. not very important
f. to anger
g. a bonus
h. too easy, liberal
i. to accuse
j. morals, worth, principles
k. ongoing, non stop
l. sharp, wise
m. poor
n. trespass
o. a leaning

IV.) ***Puzzle work.*** Now try the interactive puzzle. Put the CD (that came with your workbook) into the computer, and work the puzzle. A paper copy of the puzzle is also included at the end of this chapter.

incidental	inclination	incentive	incessant	incisive
indigent	indulgent	incorporate	indict	induce
initiate	integrity	infringe	infuriate	innovation

V.)   Write the correct new word in each sentence below:

1. There is a ten-dollar _incentive_ if you finish your work early.
2. The _incessant_ arguing in Congress left everyone exhausted.
3. Tony's contribution to the project was very _incidental_ since he rarely contributed anything to the group effort.
4. Monica's ideas were very _incisive_ and quickly adopted by the committee.
5. My first _inclination_ , when I hear someone choking, is to hit him or her on the back.
6. The seamstress tried to _incorporate_ diamonds on the dress as part of the design.
7. The Grand Jury was ready to _infringe_ her for the crime.
8. His inability to find work reduced him to the status of a(n) _indict_ .
9. The doctors wanted to _infuriate_ labor for Mrs. Hill because her due date had passed.
10. The two gamblers lived a(n) _indigent_ life in Las Vegas.
11. Standing too close to another person tends to _initiate_ on their "space."
12. The uncaring politician's attitude towards the public tended to _induce_ many people.
13. I'm so shy; I depend on others to _innovation_ friendships.
14. The plasma television is a wonderful _indulgent_ .
15. Wanda showed _integrity_ when she came forth to tell the truth.

VI.) Are you ready to take the practice test? You may take the practice test as many times as you want to. Simply insert the CD that came with book into your computer, go to "My Computer", open the CD by clicking on it, find the Practice test folder, choose this chapter's practice test and begin. (You will need a sheet of paper to write your answers on.) When finished, turn back to this chapter and correct your test. The answers are in the same order as exercise II.

VI.) **Are you ready to use the words?** Write a sentence for each word.

incidental	inclination	incentive	incessant	incisive
indigent	indulgent	incorporate	indict	induce
initiate	integrity	infringe	infuriate	innovation

1. _____

2. _____

3. _____

4. _____

5. _____

6. _____

7. _____

8. _____

9. _____

10. _____

11. _____

12. _____

13. _____

14. _____

15. _____

VIII.) Your instructor may ask you to do the puzzle on the next page. It is the same as the one on your CD. You are able to do it here once or on the CD as many times as you'd like.

Across

1. encouragement, something that produces a desire to move toward a desired end.

4. to accuse of wrongdoing

5. lenient; easygoing; liberal

6. possessing morals; having principles; honoring your commitments

8. something newly created

9. unrelenting; unstoppable

10. to bring about; to cause to occur

Down

1. to go beyond the proper limits

2. a tendency; a leaning toward

3. an impoverished person; beggar

4. to make very angry

6. penetrating; sharp; clear

7. to begin

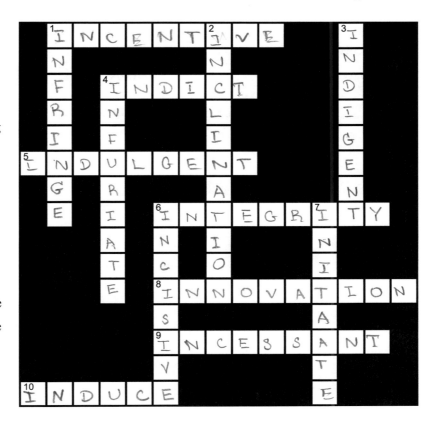

Rewrite your words

New word:		Practice writing the new word:		
Incentive				
Incessant				
Incidental				
Incisive				
Inclination				
Incorporate				
Infringe				
Indict				
Infuriate				
Indigent				
Initiate				
Induce				
Innovation				
Indulgent				
Integrity				

Improving Essential Vocabulary and Spelling Skills

I.)   ***Reflect and Connect:*** Complete the following sentences with words that are **familiar** to you and that make sense in each sentence. You may write more than one word choice for each blank space. **<u>Do not</u> look at or study the new words yet.** Answers will vary and your instructor will discuss them with you.

ingratiate   1. Through diligent work, the new lawyer was able to ___introduce___ himself with the judge.

incorrigible   2. Because of his many repeat offences, the prisoner was labeled as a(n) ___hopeless___ prisoner.

idefinite   3. The time of the meeting was ___unclear___; but we hoped that it would take place in the afternoon.

indifferent   4. When Sandra bought her new car, she was ___unconcerned___ as to the color, but very concerned about the quality of the engine.

indispensable   5. Kathy is such a good worker that she has become ___prerequisite___.

inept   6. My grandmother is a great seamstress, but I am ___clumsy___ at sewing.

inequity   7. A(n) ___injustice___ towards any group is a mistreatment aimed ultimately at all groups.

infamous   8. John Wilkes Booth is the ___disgraceful___ man who shot President Abraham Lincoln.

infimity   9. A(n) ___fair___ leader will tell the people what they need to hear, rather than what they want to hear.

ingenuous   10. Many great persons have risen above a(n) ___naive state___ that threatened to hold them physically bound.

insolvent   11. During the Great Depression, many people became ___bankrupt___ and lost everything.

incoherent   12. The accident victim was ___confused___ and the ambulance workers wondered what it was that he was trying to communicate.

inscrutable   13. She had a(n) ___impassive___ look that left everyone wondering what she was thinking.

infraction   14. A serious ___breaking___ of the law may send a person to prison.

innate   15. It seemed like Beethoven had a(n) ___common___ ability to write music because he started to do so at such a young age.

II.) ***Study the words and definitions below.*** These words and definitions are also on the enclosed CD Rom and may be printed out as study cards. The words are broken into letter groupings for easier spelling. Also, that is followed by a common definition, and common forms of the word that you might encounter. Your instructor will pronounce the words for you or you may want to use an audio dictionary for more help.

1. **ingratiate (in/gra/tiate)** 1. To commend one's self to another's good will, confidence or kindness. (It is always used as a reciprocal verb, and followed by with, before the person whose favor is sought.)
2. **incorrigible (in/corr/i/gi/ble)** 1. That which cannot be corrected or amended; bad beyond correction. 2. Too depraved to be corrected or reformed; unredeemable.
3. **indefinite (in/de/fin/ite)** 1. Not limited or defined; not determinate; not precise or certain; unsure.
4. **indifferent (in/diff/er/ent)** 1. Neutral; not inclined to one side, party or thing more than to another. 2. Unconcerned; feeling no interest, anxiety or care respecting any thing. 3. Neutral, as to good or evil. 4. Impartial; disinterested; unresponsive; cold-hearted; insensitive.
5. **indispensable (in/dis/pen/sa/ble)** 1. The state or quality of being absolutely necessary. 2. Not to be dispensed with; that cannot be omitted, remitted, or spared; absolutely necessary or requisite.
6. **inept (in/ept)** Inadequate; unfit; insufficient; incompetent.
7. **inequity (in/e/qui/ty)** Not equal; biased; not just.
8. **infamous (in/fam/ous)** 1. Branded with infamy by conviction of a crime; widely known for having done something bad. 2. Odious; detestable; held in abhorrence. 3. Of ill report, emphatically; having a reputation of the worst kind; publicly branded with odium for vice of guilt; base; scandalous; notoriously vile.

9. **infirmity (in/firm/ity)** 1. An unsound or unhealthy state of the body; weakness; feebleness. 2. Any particular disease; malady; applied rather to chronic, than to violent diseases. 3. Defect; imperfection.

10. **ingenuous (in/gen/u/ous)** Open; frank; fair; candid; free from reserve, disguise, equivocation or dissimulation.

11. **insolvent (in/sol/vent)** 1. Not having money, goods or estate sufficient to pay all debts.

12. **incoherent (in/co/her/ent)** 1. Wanting cohesion; loose; unconnected; not fixed to each other. 2. Wanting coherence or agreement; incongruous; inconsistent; having no dependence of one part on another. 2. Not able to express oneself clearly.

13. **inscrutable (in/scru/ta/ble)** That which cannot be penetrated, discovered or understood by human reason; mysterious.

14. **infraction (in/frac/tion) The act of breaking; breach; violation.**

15. **innate (inn/ate)** Inborn; native; natural; possessed at birth.

III.) ***Match the words with their definitions.*** Draw a line from the word in the first column to the definition in the second column.

d.1. ingratiate
e.2. incorrigible
a.3. indefinite
b.4. indifferent
c.5. indispensable
i.6. inept
j.7. inequity
f.8. infamous
g.9. infirmity
h.10. ingenuous
n.11. insolvent
o.12. incoherent
k.13. inscrutable
l.14. infraction
m.15. innate

a. unsure
b. not interested
c. not able to do without
d. obtain favor
e. not able to rehabilitate
f. known for evil deed
g. illness, weakness
h. candid
i. incompetent
j. unequal
k. mysterious
l. violation of law
m. inborn
n. no, or little, money
o. not understandable

IV.) ***Puzzle work.*** Now try the interactive puzzle. Put the CD (that came with your workbook) into the computer, and work the puzzle. A paper copy of the puzzle is also included at the end of this chapter.

V.) **Write the correct new word in each sentence below:**

indifferent	indispensable	incorrigible	indefinite	ingratiate
infirmity	ingenuous	inequity	infamous	inept
infraction	innate	incoherent	inscrutable	insolvent

1. Through diligent work, the new lawyer was able to ___ingartiate___ himself with the judge.

2. Because of his many repeat offences, the prisoner was labeled as a(n) ___incorrigible___ prisoner.

3. The time of the meeting was ___indefinite___; but we hoped that it would take place in the afternoon.

4. When Sandra bought her new car, she was ___indifferent___ as to the color, but very concerned about the quality of the engine.

5. Kathy is such a good worker that she has become ___indispensable___.

6. My grandmother is a great seamstress, but I am ___inept___ at sewing.

7. A(n) ___inequity___ towards any group is a mistreatment aimed ultimately at all groups.

8. John Wilkes Booth is the ___infamous___ man who shot President Abraham Lincoln.

9. A(n) ___infirmity___ leader will tell the people what they need to hear rather than what they want to hear.

10. Many great persons have risen above a(n) ___ingenous___ that threatened to hold them physically bound.

11. During the Great Depression, many people became ___insolvent___ and lost everything.

12. The accident victim was ___incoherent___ and the ambulance workers wondered what it was that he was trying to communicate.

13. She had a(n) ___inscrutable___ look that left everyone wondering what she was thinking.

14. A serious ___infraction___ of the law may send a person to prison.

15. It seemed like Beethoven had a(n) ___innate___ ability to write music because he started to do so at such a young age.

VI.) Are you ready to take the practice test? You may take the practice test as many times as you want to. Simply insert the CD that came with book into your computer, go to "My Computer", open the CD by clicking on it, find the Practice test folder, choose this chapter's practice test and begin. (You will need a sheet of paper to write your answers on.) When finished, turn back to this chapter and correct your test. The answers are in the same order as exercise II.

VI.) **Are you ready to use the words?** Write a sentence for each word.

ingratiate	incorrigible	indefinite	indifferent	indispensable
inept	inequity	infamous	infirmity	ingenuous
insolvent	incoherent	inscrutable	infraction	innate

1. _____

2. _____

3. _____

4. _____

5. _____

6. _____

7. _____

8. _____

9. _____

10. _____

11. _____

12. _____

13. _____

14. _____

15. _____

VIII.) Your instructor may ask you to do the puzzle on the next page. It is the same as the one on your CD. You are able to do it here once or on the CD as many times as you'd like.

Across

1. not certain; unsure

2. not equal; biased

6. naive; gullible; lacking sophistication

10. widely known for having done something bad

11. not able to dispense with; unable to do

12. unresponsive; cold-hearted; insensitive

Down

1. incompetent

3. possessed at birth; inborn

4. mysterious; difficult

5. not able to reform; unredeemable

7. violation

8. illness; weakness

9. not able to meet debts; bankrupt

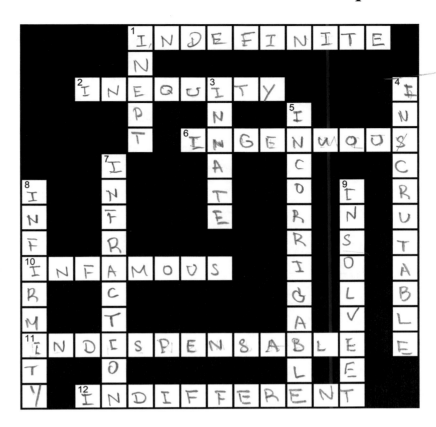

Rewrite your words

New word:		Practice writing the new word:		

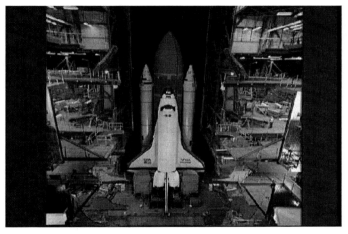

Improving Essential Vocabulary and Spelling Skills

I.) *Reflect and Connect:* Complete the following sentences with words that are **familiar** to you and that make sense in each sentence. You may write more than one word choice for each blank space. **Do not** look at or study the new words yet. Answers will vary and your instructor will discuss them with you.

precedent
1. When someone infringes on one of your rights, it sets a dangerous ___example___ for future infringements.

preclude
2. The founders of the United States hoped to ___restrain___ tyrants taking control of our government by setting up a system of checks and balances.

preconception
3. When a person has a strong ___presumption___, rather than the facts, that person is easily misled and hard to change.

predecessor
4. Bill Clinton was a ___former president___ of George W. Bush since his term in office came first.

predominant
5. The ___prime___ mood in our country is that people would like to pay fewer taxes.

premonition
6. I had a ___suspicion___ that things would work out.

prerequisite
7. The ___prerequisite___ for this job is to have a degree in Biology.

prevalent
8. Unfortunately, incompetence is ___typical___ in the world today.

pretentious
9. The King was considered a very ___selfish___ person who thought he deserved everything and his subjects deserved very little.

10. We hope that justice will ___carry through___, and that evildoers will receive the punishment they deserve.

prerogative
11. In the United States, it is the ___decision___ of the President, with the advice of the Senate, to ratify treaties.

pretense
12. Sonya put on the ___display___ of being rich, but she was living on credit cards.

prestigious
13. Frederick Douglass was given a very ___respected___ role as Ambassador to Haiti.

irrefutable
14. The truth is often ___accurate___, but some try to deny the truth anyway.

irresolute
15. Walter's actions seemed very ___doubtful___ because he was always changing his mind.

II.) ***Study the words and definitions below.*** These words and definitions are also on the enclosed CD Rom and may be printed out as study cards. The words are broken into letter groupings for easier spelling. Also, that is followed by a common definition, and common forms of the word that you might encounter. Your instructor will pronounce the words for you or you may want to use an audio dictionary for more help.

precedent	preclude	preconception	predecessor	predominant
premonition	prerequisite	prevalent	pretentious	prevail
prerogative	pretense	prestigious	irrefutable	irresolute

1. **precedent (pre/ce/dent)** 1. Something done or said, that may serve as an example to authorize a subsequent act of the like kind. 2. Something in the past, such as a court decision, that serves as a model for future decisions. 3. Going before in time.
2. **preclude (pre/cl/ude)** Prevent from happening or taking place; deter; make impossible.
3. **preconception (pre/con/cep/tion)** Conception or opinion previously formed; prejudice; bias.
4. **predecessor (pre/de/cess/or)** A person who has preceded another in the same office.
5. **predominant (pre/dom/i/nant)** Prevalent over others; superior in strength, influence or authority; greatest importance; highest position.
6. **premonition (pre/mon/i/tion)** **A** warning in advance; prophecy, inner feeling beforehand, intuition.
7. **prerequisite (pre/re/quis/ite)** Previously required or necessary to something that follows.
8. **prevalent (pre/va/lent)** 1. Widespread; 2. Predominant; most generally received or current; widely accepted; extensively existing; common.

9. **pretentious (pre/ten/tious)** Pompous; stuck-up, proud; snobbish, selfish.
10. **prevail (pre/vail)** 1. To overcome; to gain the victory or superiority; to gain the advantage; triumph. 2. To be in force; to have effect; power or influence. 3. To be predominant; to extend over with force or effect. 4. To gain or have predominant influence; to operate with effect. 5. To persuade or induce. 6. To succeed. 7. to overcome.
11. **prerogative (pre/rog/i/tive)** 1. An exclusive or peculiar privilege.
12. **pretense (pre/tense)** 1. A holding out, or offering to others, something false or feigned; a presenting to others, either in words or actions, a false or hypocritical appearance, usually with a view to conceal what is real, and thus to deceive; guise; masquerade; facade; false show.
13. **prestigious (pres/tig/ious)** Possessing prominence or influential status; highly esteemed; highly respected, important, distinguished.
14. **irrefutable (ir/re/fu/ta/ble)** 1. Not able to refute; undeniable; 2. obvious.
15. **irresolute (ir/res/o/lute)** Not determined; indecisive; not sure of how to act or proceed; wavering, changeable.

III.) *Match the words with their definitions.* Draw a line from the word in the first column to the definition in the second column.

b 1. precedent   a. greatest importance
c 2. preclude   b. a model
e. 3. preconception   c. prevent
d 4. predecessor   d. ancestor
a. 5. predominant   e. prejudice, bias
g. 6. premonition   f. to overcome
h. 7. prerequisite   g. advance feeling
j. 8. prevalent   h. required beforehand
   9. pretentious   i. vain
f. 10. prevail   j. widespread, common
l. 11. prerogative   k. uncertain
m. 12. pretense   l. choice
o. 13. prestigious   m. falseness
n. 14. irrefutable   n. not able to dispute
k 15. irresolute   o. honorable

IV.) *Puzzle work.* Now try the interactive puzzle. Put the CD (that came with your workbook) into the computer, and work the puzzle. A paper copy of the puzzle is also included at the end of this chapter.

V.)   Write the correct new word in each sentence below:

predominant	precedent	preclude	predecessor	preconception
prevail	premonition	prerequisite	pretentious	prevalent
irresolute	prerogative	pretense	irrefutable	prestigious

1. When someone infringes on one of your rights, it sets a dangerous _precedent_ for future infringements.
2. The founders of the United States hoped to _preclude_ tyrants taking control of our government by setting up a system of checks and balances.
3. When a person has a strong _preconception_, rather than the facts, that person is easily misled and hard to change.
4. Bill Clinton was a _predecessor_ of George W. Bush since his term in office came first.
5. The _predominant_ mood in our country is that people would like to pay fewer taxes.
6. I had a _premonition_ that things would work out.
7. The _prerequisite_ for this job is to have a degree in Biology.
8. Unfortunately, incompetence is _prevalent_ in the world today.
9. The King was considered a very _pretentious_ person who thought he deserved everything and his subjects deserved very little.
10. We hope that justice will _prevail_, and that evildoers will receive the punishment they deserve.
11. In the United States, it is the _prerogative_ of the President, with the advice of the Senate, to ratify treaties.
12. Sonya put on the _pretense_ of being rich, but she was living on credit cards.
13. Frederick Douglass was given a very _prestigious_ role as Ambassador to Haiti.
14. The truth is often _irrefutable_ but some try to deny the truth anyway.
15. Walter's actions seemed very _irresolute_ because he was always changing his mind.

VI.) Are you ready to take the practice test? You may take the practice test as many times as you want to. Simply insert the CD that came with book into your computer, go to "My Computer", open the CD by clicking on it, find the Practice test folder, choose this chapter's practice test and begin. (You will need a sheet of paper to write your answers on.) When finished, turn back to this chapter and correct your test. The answers are in the same order as exercise II.

VI.) **Are you ready to use the words?** Write a sentence for each word.

precedent	preclude	preconception	predecessor	predominant
premonition	prerequisite	prevalent	pretentious	prevail
prerogative	pretense	prestigious	irrefutable	irresolute

1. _____

2. _____

3. _____

4. _____

5. _____

6. _____

7. _____

8. _____

9. _____

10. _____

11. _____

12. _____

13. _____

14. _____

15. _____

VIII.) Your instructor may ask you to do the puzzle on the next page. It is the same as the one on your CD. You are able to do it here once or on the CD as many times as you'd like.

Across

4. not determined; indecisive; not sure of how to act or proceed

6. privilege; preference; right

7. a warning in advance; prophecy

8. not able to refute; undeniable

9. triumph; attain victory

Down

1. prejudice; bias

2. required beforehand

3. something in the past, such as a court decision, that serves as a model for future decisions

5. prevent, deter, make impossible

6. widely accepted; common

7. guise; masquerade; facade; false show

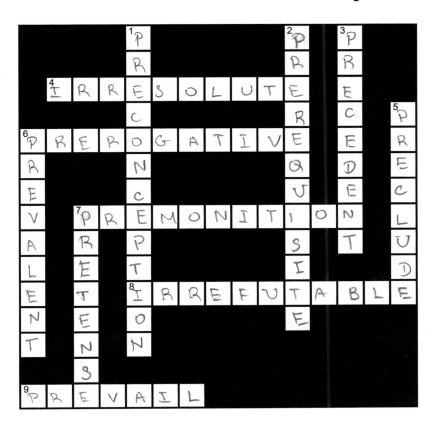

Rewrite your words

New word:		Practice writing the new word:		
Precedent				
Preclude				
Preconception				
Predecessor				
Predominant				
Premonition				
Prerequisite				
prevalent				
pretentious				
prevail				
prerogative				
pretense				
prestigious				
irrefutable				
irresolute				

Improving Essential Vocabulary and Spelling Skills

I.)   ***Reflect and Connect:*** Complete the following sentences with words that are **familiar** to you and that make sense in each sentence. You may write more than one word choice for each blank space. **Do not** look at or study the new words yet. Answers will vary and your instructor will discuss them with you.

intercede **1.** An Independent Counselor was asked to ____speak____ when the union and the company executives could not come to an agreement over the issues that caused the strike.

interference **2.** There was ___conflict___ through the shortwave radio, and not all communications could be understood.

interim **3.** The Lieutenant Governor was selected to govern during the ___temporary___ period until an election could be held.

intermittent **4.** Does your automobile have ___shifting___ wipers?

intervene **5.** The police officer decided to ___settle___ in the domestic argument in order to restore calm.

procrastinate **6.** Many students ___procrastinate___ when there is a paper is due and they try to write it at the last moment possible.

profane **7.** The way the sacred site was destroyed seemed to display a(n) ___abusive___ attitude by the enemy.

propaganda **8.** **Many people** know that many commercials for public office are nothing more than ___advertisement___.

proponent **9.** Elisa is a(n) ___supporter___ of controlling pesticides.

prospects **10.** Your employment ___anticipation___ are good if you earn a degree.

proximity **11.** The suspect was in the ___concurrence___ of the crime scene.

prodigal **12.** Do you know the story of the ___prodigal___ son who wasted his inheritance, yet was forgiven by his father?

prodigious **13.** Having a ___colossal___ amount of money doesn't guarantee happiness.

propriety **14.** The ___order___ of the formal gathering required men to wear tuxedos and ladies to wear formal gowns.

prominent **15.** One of the ___remarkable___ leaders of the country was honored with a retirement dinner.

II.) ***Study the words and definitions below.*** These words and definitions are also on the enclosed CD Rom and may be printed out as study cards. The words are broken into letter groupings for easier spelling. Also, that is followed by a common definition, and common forms of the word that you might encounter. Your instructor will pronounce the words for you or you may want to use an audio dictionary for more help.

1. **intercede (inter/cede)** To mediate; to interpose; to make intercession; to act between parties with a view to reconcile those who differ or contend; to plead on another's behalf.
2. **interference (inter/fer/ence)** 1. Interposition; an intermeddling; mediation. 2. A clashing or collision. 3. intrusiveness; 4. static.
3. **interim (in/ter/im)** Intermission; recess; interlude; waiting period.
4. **intermittent (in/ter/mitt/ent)** Ceasing at intervals; on and off from time to time; irregular; not continuous.
5. **intervene (inter/vene)** 1. To come, or be, between persons or things; to be situated between. 2. To come between points or time or events.
6. **procrastinate (pro/cras/tin/ate)** To put off from day to day; to delay; to defer to a future time.
7. **profane (pro/fane)** 1. Irreverent to any thing sacred; applied to persons. 2. Irreverent; proceeding from a contempt of sacred things; irreligious attitude.
8. **propaganda (pro/pa/gan/da)** 1. The spreading of biased information. 2. The biased information.
9. **proponent (pro/pon/ent)** Supporter; advocate.
10. **prospects (pros/pects)** 1. Possibilities. 2. Probabilities; 3. opportunities.
11. **proximity (prox/im/ity)** 1. The state of being next to; 2. immediate nearness either in place, blood or alliance; 3. vicinity, area.

12. prodigal (prod/i/gal) 1. Given to extravagant expenditures; expending money or other things without necessity; profuse, lavish; wasteful; not frugal or economical. 2. Profuse, lavish; expended to excess or without necessity; very liberal.

13. prodigious (pro/dig/ious) 1. Very great; huge; enormous in size, quantity, extent. 2. Wonderful; astonishing; such as may seem a prodigy; monstrous; portentous.

14. propriety (pro/pri/ety) 1. Fitness; suitableness; appropriateness; consonance with established principles, rules or customs; justness; accuracy. 2. Property; peculiar or exclusive right of possession; ownership. 3. Proper state; civility; decorum; etiquette.

15. prominent (prom/in/ent) 1. Eminent; distinguished above others; as a prominent character. 2. Noticeable; conspicuous; principal; most visible or striking to the eye.

III.) *Match the words with their definitions.* Draw a line from the word in the first column to the definition in the second column.

b.	**1. intercede**	**a. time between**
d.	**2. interference**	**b. mediator**
a.	**3. interim**	**c. to come between**
e.	**4. intermittent**	**d. intrusiveness**
c.	**5. intervene**	**e. not continuous**
g.	**6. procrastinate**	**f. biased information**
h.	**7. profane**	**g. to keep putting off**
f.	**8. propaganda**	**h. irreligious**
j.	**9. proponent**	**i. chances for success**
i.	**10. prospects**	**j. supporter**
l.	**11. proximity**	**k. enormous**
m.	**12. prodigal**	**l. nearness**
k.	**13. prodigious**	**m. wasteful**
o.	**14. propriety**	**n. eminent**
n.	**15. prominent**	**o. civility, etiquette**

IV.) *Puzzle work.* Now try the interactive puzzle. Put the CD (that came with your workbook) into the computer, and work the puzzle. A paper copy of the puzzle is also included at the end of this chapter.

V.)   Write the correct new word in each sentence below:

interim	intercede	interference	intervene	intermittent
propaganda	procrastinate	profane	prospects	proponent
prodigious	proximity	prodigal	prominent	propriety

1. An Independent Counselor was asked to __intercede__ when the union and the company executives could not come to an agreement over the issues that caused the strike.
2. There was __interference__ through the shortwave radio, and not all communications could be understood.
3. The Lieutenant Governor was selected to govern during the __interim__ period until an election could be held.
4. Does your automobile have __intermittent__ wipers?
5. The police officer decided to __intervene__ in the domestic argument in order to restore calm.
6. Many students __procrastinate__ when there is a paper is due and they try to write it at the last moment possible.
7. The way the sacred site was destroyed seemed to display a(n) __profane__ attitude by the enemy.
8. Many People know that many commercials for public office are nothing more than __propaganda__.
9. Elisa is a(n) __proponent__ of controlling pesticides.
10. Your employment __prospects__ are good if you earn a degree.
11. The suspect was in the __proximity__ of the crime scene.
12. Do you know the story of the __prodigal__ son who wasted his inheritance, yet was forgiven by his father?
13. Having a __prodigious__ amount of money doesn't guarantee happiness.
14. The __propriety__ of the formal gathering required men to wear tuxedos and ladies to wear formal gowns.
15. One of the __prominent__ leaders of the country was honored with a retirement dinner.

VI.) Are you ready to take the practice test? You may take the practice test as many times as you want to. Simply insert the CD that came with book into your computer, go to "My Computer", open the CD by clicking on it, find the Practice test folder, choose this chapter's practice test and begin. (You will need a sheet of paper to write your answers on.) When finished, turn back to this chapter and correct your test. The answers are in the same order as exercise II.

VI.) Are you ready to use the words? Write a sentence for each word.

interim	intermittent	intervene	intercede	interference
propaganda	proponent	prospects	procrastinate	profane
prodigious	propriety	prominent	proximity	prodigal

1. _____

2. _____

3. _____

4. _____

5. _____

6. _____

7. _____

8. _____

9. _____

10. _____

11. _____

12. _____

13. _____

14. _____

15. _____

VIII.) Your instructor may ask you to do the puzzle on the next page. It is the same as the one on your CD. You are able to do it here once or on the CD as many times as you'd like.

Across

2. supporter

4. wasteful spending

6. the spreading of biased information; the biased information

7. on and off from time to time; irregular

8. something or someone causing interference

9. intermission; recess; interlude

Down

1. to plead on another's behalf; mediator

2. noticeable; conspicuous; eminent

3. to keep putting off until a later time

4. enormous; extremely large

5. contempt or irreverence for sacred things

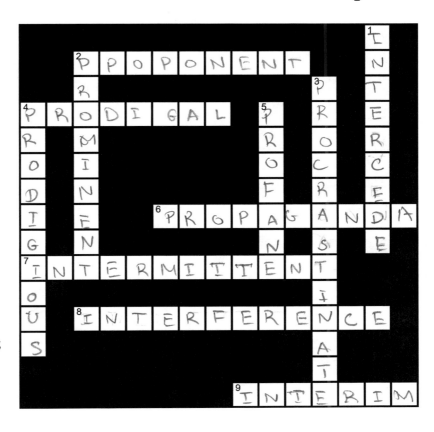

Rewrite your words

New word:		Practice writing the new word:		

Improving Essential Vocabulary and Spelling Skills

I.)   *Reflect and Connect:* Complete the following sentences with words that are **familiar** to you and that make sense in each sentence. You may write more than one word choice for each blank space. **Do not** look at or study the new words yet. Answers will vary and your instructor will discuss them with you.

benefactor   **1.** An anonymous ___promoter___ gave a large amount of money to help with after school programs.

benevolent   **2.** Giving financial help to those in need is a very ___humane___ thing to do.

chronic   **3.** A person with a ___relentless___ illness will eventually need to get help from the medical establishment.

chronological **4.** A timeline is constructed in ___sequential___ order.

averse   **5.** Some persons are very ___reluctant___ to eating vegetables, but vegetables are considered essential to good health.

coalesce   **6.** The General decided to ___merge___ his troops into one large group.

coerce   **7.** I had to ___force___ my dog to obey me by giving it treats.

coherent   **8.** The speech was well planned and delivered in a very ___articulate___ manner.

malevolent **9.** The dictator had a very ___hostile___ attitude towards humanity.

malignant **10.** Sarah was relieved to hear that the tumor was not ___lethal___.

malign   **11.** Often politicians speak evil of their opponents, and therefore hope to ___destroy___ the opposition's character in the minds of the voters.

malpractice **12.** It is always wise to check a doctor's record for ___misconducts___ suits before going for services.

antagonist **13.** Most works of literature have at least one protagonist and at least one ___antagonist___.

antidote   **14.** When walking in the woods, it is wise to carry a(n) ___antidote___ to snake bites.

blasé   **15.** After working on the assembly line for thirty years, Andrea had a very ___weary___ attitude about going to work.

II.) *Study the words and definitions below.* These words and definitions are also on the enclosed CD Rom and may be printed out as study cards. The words are broken into letter groupings for easier spelling. Also, that is followed by a common definition, and common forms of the word that you might encounter. Your instructor will pronounce the words for you or you may want to use an audio dictionary for more help.

1. **benefactor (bene/fac/tor)** He who confers a benefit, especially one who makes charitable contributions either for public institutions or for private use. **(Benefactress – same as above but a female.)**
2. **benevolent (bene/vo/lent)** Having a disposition to do good; possessing love for mankind, and a desire to promote their prosperity and happiness; kind; charitable; generous; altruistic.
3. **chronic (chron/ic)** Continuing to occur over time.
4. **chronological (chron/o/log/i/cal)** Containing an account of events in the order of time; occurring in a logical time order.
5. **averse (a/ver/se)** 1. Disliking; unwilling; having a repugnance of mind. 2. Unfavorable; indisposed. 3. Opposed to.
6. **coalesce (co/al/esce)** 1. To grow together; to unite, as separate bodies, or separate parts, into one body. 2. To unite and adhere in one body or mass, by spontaneous approximation or attraction. 3. To unite in society.
7. **coerce (co/er/ce)** 1. To restrain by force; to keep from acting, or transgressing, particularly by moral force. 2. To compel; to constrain.
8. **coherent (co/her/ent)** 1. Sticking together; cleaving. 2. Connected; united, by some relation in form or order; clear; understandable. 3. Consistent; having an agreement of parts.
9. **malevolent (mal/e/vo/lent)** 1. Having an evil disposition towards another or others; wishing evil to others; ill disposed, or disposed to injure others; malicious. 2. Bringing calamity.

10. malignant (mal/ig/nant) 1. Dangerous to life; life threatening. 2. Malicious; having extreme malevolence or enmity. 3. Virulent. 4. Extremely heinous.

11. malign (mal/ign) 1. To defame. 2. Unfavorable; tending to injure. 3. To regard with envy or malice; to treat with extreme enmity; to injure maliciously. 4. Having a very evil disposition towards others; harboring violent hatred or enmity; malicious.

12. malpractice (mal/prac/tice) 1. Improper or negligent practice of medicine. 2. Practice contrary to established rules.

13. antagonist (an/ta/gon/ist) 1. An opponent in controversy; adversary. 2. One who contends with another in combat.

14. antidote (anti/dote) A medicine to counteract the effects of poison, or of any thing noxious taken into the stomach; corrective; neutralizing agent.

15. blasé (bla/sé) Producing boredom due to overuse or overexposure.

III.) *Match the words with their definitions.* Draw a line from the word in the first column to the definition in the second column.

c .1. benefactor   a. occurring continually
d .2. benevolent   b. logical time order
a .3. chronic   c. one who gives
b .4. chronological   d. good, charitable
e .5. averse   e. opposed to
h .6. coalesce   f. clearly understood
i .7. coerce   g. wishing harm
f .8. coherent   h. to bring together
g .9. malevolent   i. to force
j .10. malignant   j. life threatening
m .11. malign   k. opponent
o .12. malpractice   l. remedy for poison
k .13. antagonist   m. speak evil of
l .14. antidote   n. bored
n .15. blasé   o. incompetence in medicine

IV.) *Puzzle work.* Now try the interactive puzzle. Put the CD (that came with your workbook) into the computer, and work the puzzle. A paper copy of the puzzle is also included at the end of this chapter.

V.) Write the correct new word in each sentence below:

averse	chronic	benefactor	benevolent	chronological
malignant	coherent	coalesce	coerce	malevolent
blasé	antagonist	malign	malpractice	antidote

1. An anonymous ____benefactor____ gave a large amount of money to help with after school programs.
2. Giving financial help to those in need is a very ____benevolent____ thing to do.
3. A person with a ____chronic____ illness will eventually need to get help from the medical establishment.
4. A timeline is constructed in ____chronological____ order.
5. Some persons are very ____averse____ to eating vegetables, but vegetables are considered essential to good health.
6. The General decided to ____coalesce____ his troops into one large group.
7. I had to ____coerce____ my dog to obey me by giving it treats.
8. The speech was well planned and delivered in a very ____coherent____ manner.
9. The dictator had a very ____malvolent____ attitude towards humanity.
10. Sarah was relieved to hear that the tumor was not ____malignant____.
11. Often politicians speak evil of their opponents, and therefore hope to ____malign____ the opposition's character in the minds of the voters.
12. It is always wise to check a doctor's record for ____malpractice____ suits before going for services.
13. Most works of literature have at least one protagonist and at least one ____antagonist____.
14. When walking in the woods, it is wise to carry a(n) ____antidote____ to snake bites.
15. After working on the assembly line for thirty years, Andrea had a very ____blasé____ attitude about going to work.

VI.) Are you ready to take the practice test? You may take the practice test as many times as you want to. Simply insert the CD that came with book into your computer, go to "My Computer", open the CD by clicking on it, find the Practice test folder, choose this chapter's practice test and begin. (You will need a sheet of paper to write your answers on.) When finished, turn back to this chapter and correct your test. The answers are in the same order as exercise II.

VII.) Are you ready to use the words? Write a sentence for each word.

chronic	chronological	benefactor	benevolent	averse
coherent	malevolent	coalesce	coerce	malignant
antagonist	antidote	malign	malpractice	blasé

1. _____
_____

2. _____
_____

3. _____
_____

4. _____
_____

5. _____
_____

6. _____
_____

7. _____
_____

8. _____
_____

9. _____
_____

10._____
_____

11._____
_____

12._____
_____

13._____
_____

14._____
_____

15._____
_____

VIII.) Your instructor may ask you to do the puzzle on the next page. It is the same as the one on your CD. You are able to do it here once or on the CD as many times as you'd like.

Across

1. to speak evil of

2. continuing to occur over time

4. unite; merge; bond

10. opposition; distaste

11. charitable; generous

12. occurring in logical time order

Down

1. improper or negligent practice of medicine

3. to force; compel; pressure

5. adversary, opponent; competitor

6. producing boredom due to overuse or overexposure

7. exhibiting ill will; wishing harm to others; malicious

8. one who generously gives

9. clear; understandable

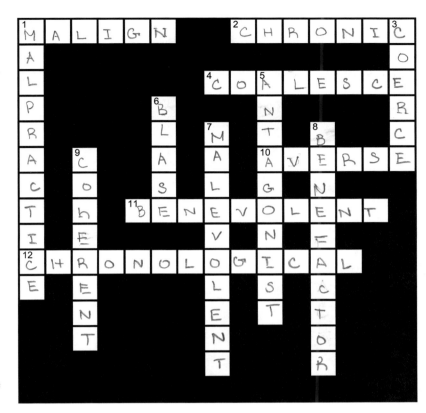

Rewrite your words

New word:		Practice writing the new word:		
Benefactor				
Benevolent				
Chronic				
Chronological				
Averse				
Coealesce				
Coerce				
Concrent				
Malavolent				
Milgnant				
Malign				
Malpractice				
Antagonist				
Antidote				
blasé				

Improving Essential Vocabulary and Spelling Skills

I.)   ***Reflect and Connect:*** Complete the following sentences with words that are **familiar** to you and that make sense in each sentence. You may write more than one word choice for each blank space. **<u>Do not</u> look at or study the new words yet.** Answers will vary and your instructor will discuss them with you.

affiliate   1. The people that you ___hang out___ with, often, will have an influence on your life.

alleviate   2. Aspirin is known to ___lessen___ headache pain.

altruistic   3. Janelle is very ___benevolent___ and often gives to local charities.

ambivalent   4. Bill was ___wavering___ in answering the questions put to him and no one understood his answers.

animosity   5. It's not good governing when political parties show great ___hostile___ towards their opponents.

appease   6. Sometimes, in the interest of peace, we need to ___subdue___ our rivals even though we know they are wrong.

arbitrary   7. No one would want to go before a judge whose rule was always ___inconsistent___.

aspire   8. It is good to ___strive___ to greatness, but we must know our limitations too.

attribute   9. His best ___quality___ is his charming smile.

benign   10. Sahib was relieved when the doctor told him that the tumor was ___harmless___.

blatant   11. Speeding through the city at one hundred miles per hour is a ___clear___ violation of the law.

charisma   12. It takes a lot of ___appeal___ to be a good politician.

diversion   13. Most people, who work hard, will need a(n) ___alteration___ to break up their routine.

divulge   14. The detective told her to ___admit___ everything she knew about the crime.

eccentric   15. My aunt is a(n) ___abnormal___ woman who has dyed pink hair and wears mismatched colors.

II.)   *Study the words and definitions below.* These words and definitions are also on the enclosed CD Rom and may be printed out as study cards. The words are broken into letter groupings for easier spelling. Also, that is followed by a common definition, and common forms of the word that you might encounter. Your instructor will pronounce the words for you or you may want to use an audio dictionary for more help.

1. **affiliate (aff/il/iate)** To closely associate with a group or society.
2. **alleviate (all/ev/iate)** To relieve; to lessen the magnitude of.
3. **altruistic (al/tru/is/tic)** Generous; possessing a giving nature.
4. **ambivalent am/biv/a/lent)** Having an unclear meaning, vague.
5. **animosity (an/i/mos/ity)** Violent hatred accompanied with active opposition; active enmity; a hateful attitude; animalistic character to the behavior.
6. **appease (app/ease)** To make quiet; to calm; to reduce to a state of peace; to still; to pacify; to placate.
7. **arbitrary (ar/bi/tr/ary)** 1. Depending on personal will or discretion; not governed by any fixed rules; biased. 2. Despotic; absolute in power; having no external control.
8. **aspire (as/pire)** 1. To aim at something elevated; to rise or tower with desire; working toward a lofty goal. 2. To desire with eagerness; to strongly desire greatness, nobleness or spirituality.
9. **attribute (att/ri/bute)** 1. That which is attributed; that which is considered as belonging to, or inherent in; a characteristic; a talent. 2. Quality; characteristic disposition. 3. Reputation; honor.
10. **benign (be/nign)** 1. Kind; of a kind disposition; gracious; favorable; friendly; not harmful. 2. Generous; liberal. 3. Favorable; having a salutary influence. 4. Wholesome; not pernicious. 5. Favorable; not malignant; not cancerous.

11.blatant (bla/tant) Obvious; clear; unmistakable; flagrant.

12.charisma (char/is/ma) A pleasant, charming personality that draws others into admiration.

13.diversion (di/ver/sion) 1. The act of turning aside from any course; a turning away from the ordinary; a distraction. 2. That which diverts; that which turns or draws the mind from care, business or study, and thus relaxes and amuses; sport; play; pastime; whatever relaxes the mind. 3. In war, the act of drawing the attention and force of an enemy from the point where the principal attack is to be made, as by an attack or alarm on one wing of an army, when the other wing or center is intended for the principal attack. The enemy, if deceived, is thus induced to withdraw a part of his force from the part where his foe intends to make the main impression.

14.divulge (di/vulge) 1. To make public; to tell or make known something before private or secret; to reveal; to disclose. 2. To declare by a public act; to proclaim.

15.eccentric (ecc/en/tric) 1. Deviating from stated methods, usual practice or established forms or laws; irregular; anomalous, departing from the usual course; odd; unusual. 2. Deviating or departing from the center.

III.) *Match the words with their definitions.* Draw a line from the word in the first column to the definition in the second column.

d.1. affiliate   a. unclear meaning

e.2. alleviate   b. intense hatred

c.3. altruistic   c. generous, a giving nature

a.4. ambivalent   d. to associate with

b.5. animosity   e. to relieve pain

i.6. appease   f. a characteristic

j.7. arbitrary   g. friendly, not harmful

h.8. aspire   h. toward a lofty goal

f.9. attribute   i. to give in to, placate

g.10. benign   j. biased, no rules

n.11. blatant   k. to reveal

o.12. charisma   l. odd, weird

m.13. diversion   m. distraction

k.14. divulge   n. obvious

l.15. eccentric   o. charming character

IV.) *Puzzle work.* Now try the interactive puzzle. Put the CD (that came with your workbook) into the computer, and work the puzzle. A paper copy of the puzzle is also included at the end of this chapter.

V.)   Write the correct new word in each sentence below:

altruistic	animosity	affiliate	alleviate	ambivalent
aspire	benign	appease	arbitrary	attribute
diversion	eccentric	blatant	charisma	divulge

1. The people that you __affiliate__ with, often, will have an influence on your life.
2. Aspirin is known to __alleviate__ headache pain.
3. Janelle is very __altruistic__ and often gives to local charities.
4. Bill was __ambivalent__ in answering the questions put to him and no one understood his answers.
5. It's not good governing when political parties show great __animosity__ towards their opponents.
6. Sometimes, in the interest of peace, we need to __appease__ our rivals even though we know they are wrong.
7. No one would want to go before a judge whose rule was always __arbitrary__.
8. It is good to __aspire__ to greatness, but we must know our limitations too.
9. His best __attribute__ is his charming smile.
10. Sahib was relieved when the doctor told him that the tumor was __benign__.
11. Speeding through the city at one hundred miles per hour is a __blatant__ violation of the law.
12. It takes a lot of __charisma__ to be a good politician.
13. Most people, who work hard, will need a __diversion__ to break up their routine.
14. The detective told her to __divulge__ every thing she knew about the crime.
15. My aunt is a(n) __eccentric__ women who has died pink hair and wears mismatched colors.

VI.) Are you ready to take the practice test? You may take the practice test as many times as you want to. Simply insert the CD that came with book into your computer, go to "My Computer", open the CD by clicking on it, find the Practice test folder, choose this chapter's practice test and begin. (You will need a sheet of paper to write your answers on.) When finished, turn back to this chapter and correct your test. The answers are in the same order as exercise II.

VII.) Are you ready to use the words? Write a sentence for each word.

ambivalent	altruistic	alleviate	affiliate	animosity
attribute	aspire	arbitrary	appease	benign
divulge	diversion	charisma	blatant	eccentric

1. _____

2. _____

3. _____

4. _____

5. _____

6. _____

7. _____

8. _____

9. _____

10. _____

11. _____

12. _____

13. _____

14. _____

15. _____

VIII.) Your instructor may ask you to do the puzzle on the next page. It is the same as the one on your CD. You are able to do it here once or on the CD as many times as you'd like.

Across

2. working toward a lofty goal

4. to relieve; to lessen

6. a pleasant, charming character

9. obvious; clear; unmistakable

11. a turning away from the ordinary

12. to associate with

Down

1. an unclear meaning

2. to give in order to placate

3. generous; a giving nature

4. a characteristic; talent

5. odd; unusual

7. no rule or reason; biased

8. friendly; not cancerous

10. to reveal

Rewrite your words

New word:		Practice writing the new word:		

Improving Essential Vocabulary and Spelling Skills

I.) *Reflect and Connect:* Complete the following sentences with words that are **familiar** to you and that make sense in each sentence. You may write more than one word choice for each blank space. **Do not look at or study the new words yet.** Answers will vary and your instructor will discuss them with you.

empathy 1. Sally had a feeling of ___understanding___ for Margaret's pain because she had also given birth to twins.

escalate 2. The fighting began to ___magnify___ and more troops were sent in to the battle.

epitome 3. Tiger Woods is the ___illustration___ of a golf professional.

euphemism 4. A(n) ___pretense___ for the word "died" is "passed away" because it doesn't sound so harsh.

facade 5. The ___structure___ of the building was deteriorating so badly that bricks were falling to the street.

fallible 6. We are all ___imperfect___ and therefore we should forgive others who make mistakes.

feasible 7. The inventor's ideas seemed ___reasonable___ and they began production on the new product.

fluctuate 8. The stock market is a risky investment because it tends to ___vary___ a lot.

Hypothetical 9. Scientists taught the earth revolving around the sun as a ___doubtful___ teaching until later evidence proved it to be true.

gradualism 10. Many politicians use a technique known as ___gradualism___ whereby change is made in very slow, almost imperceptible, increments.

inalienable 11. The Declaration of Independence states that we have the ___basic___ rights of life, liberty and the pursuit of happiness.

credible 12. The jury listened to the evidence and later discussed whether it was ___sincere___ or not.

cryptic 13. Many mystery stories contain ___vague___ clues that must be figured out in order to solve the crime.

digress 14. A powerful speech should not ___depart___ from the topic.

delimme 15. Monica had a ___problem___ - should she stay with Bill or choose Hernando instead?

II.) *Study the words and definitions below.* These words and definitions are also on the enclosed CD Rom and may be printed out as study cards. The words are broken into letter groupings for easier spelling. Also, that is followed by a common definition, and common forms of the word that you might encounter. Your instructor will pronounce the words for you or you may want to use an audio dictionary for more help.

1. **empathy (em/pa/thy)** Insight; compassion; sympathy.
2. **escalate (es/ca/late)** To increase or intensify.
3. **epitome (e/pi/tome)** A perfect example; ideal.
4. **euphemism (eu/phe/mism)** A representation of good qualities; particularly in rhetoric, a figure in which a harsh or indelicate word or expression is softened, or rather by which a delicate word or expression is substituted for one which is offensive to good manners or to delicate ears; the substitution of mild of vague words or terms for those that are considered too harsh.
5. **facade (fa/cade) 1.** The face of a building; face. 2. A false front; phoniness.
6. **fallible (fall/i/ble)** 1. Liable to fail or mistake; that may err or be deceived in judgment. 2. Liable to error. 3. Able to fall; weakly supported argument.
7. **feasible (feas/i/ble)** That may be done, performed, executed or effected; practicable.; possible; likely to function or work.
8. **fluctuate (fluc/tu/ate)** 1. To move now in one direction and now in another; to be wavering or unsteady. 2. To be irresolute or undetermined. 3. To rise and fall; to be in an unsettled state. 4. To move as a wave; to roll hither and thither; to wave; as a fluctuating field of air. 5. To float backward and forward, as on waves.
9. **hypothetical (hy/po/the/ti/cal)** 1. Something not proved, but assumed for the purpose of argument. 2. Theoretical; theory or ideas based on evidence. 3. Conditional; assumed without proof for the purpose of reasoning and deducing proof.

10. **gradualism (grad/u/al/ism)** Proceeding by very small steps or degrees; advancing step by step; passing from one step to another; regular and slow; almost imperceptible.

11. **inalienable (in/al/ien/able)** Not able to deny. 2. Not able to alienate. 3. Known; not foreign or strange.

12. **credible (cred/i/ble)** 1. That may be believed; worthy of credit. 2. Worthy of belief; having a claim to credit; (applied to persons).

13. **cryptic (cryp/tic)** Mysterious; coded; secret; occult.

14. **digress (di/gr/ess)** 1. To go out of the right way or common track; to deviate; in a literal sense; to stray from the main topic. 2. Literally, to step or go from the way or road; hence, to depart or wander from the main subject, design or tenor of a discourse, argument or narration; used only of speaking or writing.

15. **dilemma (di/le/mma)** 1. A difficult choice between two or more options. 2. A difficult or doubtful choice; a state of things in which evils or obstacles present themselves on every side, and it is difficult to determine what course to pursue.

III.) *Match the words with their definitions.* Write the letter of the correct definition before the number of the corresponding word choice.

c 1. empathy
c 2. escalate
a 3. epitome
e 4. euphemism
b 5. facade
h 6. fallible
i 7. feasible
f 8. fluctuate
j 9. hypothetical
k 10. inalienable
g 11. gradualism
n 12. credible
m 13. cryptic
o 14. digress
l 15. dilemma

a. perfect example
b. false front
c. compassion
d. increase
e. milder substitute word
f. unevenness
g. small incremental steps
h. able to fall, weak point
i. possible
j. theoretical
k. not foreign
l. difficult choice
m. mysterious
n. believable
o. to stray from the main topic

IV.) *Puzzle work.* Now try the interactive puzzle. Put the CD (that came with your workbook) into the computer, and work the puzzle. A paper copy of the puzzle is also included at the end of this chapter.

V.) **Write the correct new word in each sentence below:**

escalate	facade	empathy	epitome	euphemism
feasible	inalienable	fallible	fluctuate	hypothetical
credible	dilemma	gradualism	cryptic	digress

1. Sally had a feeling of ___empathy___ for Margaret's pain because she had also given birth to twins.

2. The fighting began to ___escalate___ and more troops were sent in to the battle.

3. Tiger Woods is the ___epitome___ of a golf professional.

4. A(n) ___euphemism___ for the word "died" is "passed away" because it doesn't sound so harsh.

5. The ___facade___ of the building was deteriorating so badly that bricks were falling to the street.

6. We are all ___fallible___ and therefore we should forgive others who make mistakes.

7. The inventor's ideas seemed ___feasible___ and they began production on the new product.

8. The stock market is a risky investment because it tends to ___fluctuate___ a lot.

9. Scientists taught the earth revolving around the sun as a ___hypothetical___ teaching until later evidence proved it to be definitely true.

10. Many politicians use a technique known as ___inaliable___ whereby change is made in very slow, almost imperceptible, increments.

11. The Declaration of Independence states that we have the ___gradualism___ rights of life, liberty and the pursuit of happiness.

12. The jury listened to the evidence and later discussed whether it was ___credible___ or not.

13. Many mystery stories contain ___cryptic___ clues that must be figured out in order to solve the crime.

14. A powerful speech should not ___digress___ from the topic.

15. Monica had a ___dilimma___ - should she stay with Bill or choose Hernando instead?

VI.) Are you ready to take the practice test? You may take the practice test as many times as you want to. Simply insert the CD that came with book into your computer, go to "My Computer", open the CD by clicking on it, find the Practice test folder, choose this chapter's practice test and begin. (You will need a sheet of paper to write your answers on.) When finished, turn back to this chapter and correct your test. The answers are in the same order as exercise II.

VII.) Are you ready to use the words? Write a sentence for each word.

empathy	escalate	epitome	euphemism	façade
fallible	feasible	fluctuate	hypothetical	inalienable
gradualism	credible	cryptic	digress	dilemma

1. _____

2. _____

3. _____

4. _____

5. _____

6. _____

7. _____

8. _____

9. _____

10. _____

11. _____

12. _____

13. _____

14. _____

15. _____

VIII.) Your instructor may ask you to do the puzzle on the next page. It is the same as the one on your CD. You are able to do it here once or on the CD as many times as you'd like.

Across

1. believable

3. front of building; false front

4. difficult choice

8. theoretical

9. to stray from the topic

11. not foreign

12. mysterious; hidden

13. intensify

Down

2. compassion

3. changeable

5. milder word or term

6. able to fall; weakly supported

7. in small increments

10. possible; workable

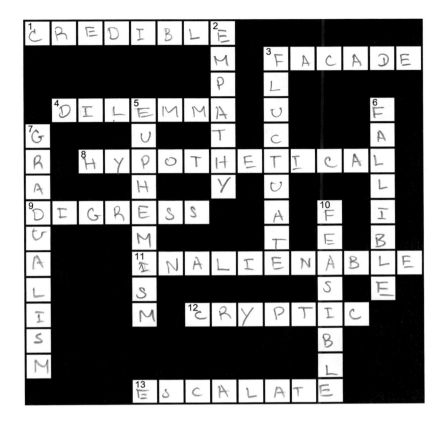

Rewrite your words

New word:	Practice writing the new word:		
Empathy			
Escalate			
epitome			
euphemism			
facade			
fallible			
feasible			
fluctuate			
Hypothetical			
inalienable			
gredualism			
credible			
oryptic			
digress			
dilemma			

Improving Essential Vocabulary and Spelling Skills

I.)   ***Reflect and Connect:*** Complete the following sentences with words that are **familiar** to you and that make sense in each sentence. You may write more than one word choice for each blank space. **<u>Do not</u> look at or study the new words yet.** Answers will vary and your instructor will discuss them with you.

diligent

1. A worker who is ____eager____ in carrying out her work is a valuable asset to an employer.

intimidate

2. The three hundred pound football player tended to ____threaten____ his opponents.

intricate

3. The lace she had on her table was a very __elaborate__ design from Denmark.

intrinsic

4. His ability to write well was not learned, but seemed to be a(n) ____innate____ part of his personality.

introspection

5. It is good to spend some time in ____meditation____ whereby you are able to look at your strengths and weaknesses.

ironic

6. It is ____cynical____ that Stewart won a trip to Hawaii since he lives in Honolulu.

jeopardize

7. Janis decided she would not ____risk____ her chances of passing the course by giving in to the temptation to cheat.

latent

8. Often, I am working with one active program on the screen while I have another sitting ____hidden____ on the taskbar.

legacy

9. The early settlers in America left us a(n) ____heritage____ of hard work, honesty, and human kindness.

longevity

10. Mary, who is 96 years old, says the secret to her __durability__ is eating steamed onions and roasted garlic every day.

lucrative

11. A(n) ____productive____ job is one that pays you well.

mediate

12. The United States tried to ____negotiate____ a peace agreement between the Palestinians and the Israelis.

mercenary

13. In nearly every war, there are ____corrupt____ soldiers who fight only because they are being paid to do so.

methodical

14. Some people are more ____organize____ in their work habits than others, and this usually produces quality work.

mortify

15. Forgetting lines during a professional performance of a play would usually ____humiliate____ the actress or actor.

II.) ***Study the words and definitions below.*** These words and definitions are also on the enclosed CD Rom and may be printed out as study cards. The words are broken into letter groupings for easier spelling. Also, that is followed by a common definition, and common forms of the word that you might encounter. Your instructor will pronounce the words for you or you may want to use an audio dictionary for more help.

1. **diligent (dil/i/gent)** 1. Steady in application to business; constant in effort or exertion to accomplish what is undertaken; attentive; industrious; not idle or negligent. 2. Steadily applied; prosecuted with care and constant effort; careful.
2. **intimidate (in/tim/i/date)** To make fearful; to inspire with fear; to dishearten; to tower over; frighten.
3. **intricate (in/tri/cate)** 1. Entangled, involved; perplexed; obscure; 2. Detailed complicated.
4. **intrinsic (in/trin/sic)** Inward; internal; hence, true; genuine; real; essential; inherent; inborn; existing at birth.
5. **introspection (in/tro/spec/tion)** A view of the inside or interior; looking inward; pondering; self-examination.
6. **ironic (i/ron/ic)** Receiving the opposite of what was expected.
7. **jeopardize (jeo/par/dize)** To expose to loss or injury; to put in harm's way.
8. **latent (la/tent)** 1. Hid; concealed; secret; not seen; not visible or apparent. 2. Active but hidden
9. **legacy (le/gacy)** 1. Tradition; 2. Inheritance; Something left by will; a particular thing; 3. A certain sum of money given by last will or testament.
10. **longevity (lon/gev/ity)** Length or duration of life; more generally, great length of life.
11. **lucrative (lu/cra/tive)** Gainful; profitable; making increase of money or goods.

12. mediate (med/i/ate) 1. Negotiate; 2. To interpose between parties, as the equal friend of each; to act indifferently between contending parties, with a view to reconciliation; to intercede.

13. mercenary (mer/cen/ary) 1. Hired; purchased by money; hireling; 2. Greedy of gain; mean; selfish; motivated only by material or monetary gain. 3. A hired soldier. 4. Moved by the love of money.

14. methodical (me/thod/i/cal) Arranged in convenient order; disposed in a just and natural manner, or in a manner to illustrate a subject, or to facilitate practical operations; orderly; systematic.

15. mortify (mor/ti/fy) 1. Embarrassment to the point of wanting to almost die, embarrass to "death." 2. To destroy the organic texture and vital functions of some part of a living animal. 3. To subdue or bring into subjection. 4. To subdue; to abase; to humble. Also: **mortified**.

III.) *Match the words with their definitions.* Write the letter of the correct definition before the number of the corresponding word choice.

a. 1. diligent
e. 2. intimidate
d. 3. intricate
b. 4. intrinsic
c. 5. introspection
i. 6. ironic
j. 7. jeopardize
f. 8. latent
g. 9. legacy
h. 10. longevity
n. 11. lucrative
o. 12. mediate
k. 13. mercenary
l. 14. methodical
m. 15. mortify

a. detailed
b. inborn
c. self examination
d. attention to detail
e. to instill fear
f. present but not active
g. inheritance
h. long life
i. not expected
j. put in danger
k. hireling, hired soldier
l. orderly
m. embarrass to "death"
n. profitable
o. to come between to solve a problem

IV.) *Puzzle work.* Now try the interactive puzzle. Put the CD (that came with your workbook) into the computer, and work the puzzle. A paper copy of the puzzle is also included at the end of this chapter.

V.) **Write the correct new word in each sentence below:**

intricate	introspection	diligent	intrinsic	intimidate
latent	longevity	ironic	legacy	jeopardize
mercenary	mortify	lucrative	methodical	mediate

1. A worker who is _____diligent_____ in carrying out her work is a valuable asset to an employer.
2. The three hundred pound football player tended to _intimidate_ his opponents.
3. The lace she had on her table was a very _intricate_ design from Denmark.
4. His ability to write well was not learned, but seemed to be a(n) _intrinsic_ part of his personality.
5. It is good to spend some time in _introspection_ whereby you are able to look at your strengths and weaknesses.
6. It is _____ironic_____ that Stewart won a trip to Hawaii since he lives in Honolulu.
7. Janis decided she would not _jeopardize_ her chances of passing the course by giving in to the temptation to cheat.
8. Often, I am working with one active program on the screen while I have another sitting _____latent_____ on the taskbar.
9. The early settlers in America left us a(n) _legacy_ of hard work, honesty, and human kindness.
10. Mary, who is 96 years old, says the secret to her _longevity_ is eating steamed onions and roasted garlic every day.
11. A(n) _____lucrative_____ job is one that pays you well.
12. The United States tried to _____mediate_____ a peace agreement between the Palestinians and the Israelis.
13. In nearly every war, there are _____mercenary_____ soldiers who fight only because they are being paid to do so.
14. Some people are more _methodical_ in their work habits than others, and this usually produces quality work.
15. Forgetting lines during a professional performance of a play would usually _____mortify_____ the actress or actor.

VI.) Are you ready to take the practice test? You may take the practice test as many times as you want to. Simply insert the CD that came with book into your computer, go to "My Computer", open the CD by clicking on it, find the Practice test folder, choose this chapter's practice test and begin. (You will need a sheet of paper to write your answers on.)

VII.) Are you ready to use the words? Write a sentence for each word.

diligent	intimidate	intricate	intrinsic	introspection
ironic	jeopardize	latent	legacy	longevity
lucrative	mediate	mercenary	methodical	mortify

1. _____

2. _____

3. _____

4. _____

5. _____

6. _____

7. _____

8. _____

9. _____

10. _____

11. _____

12. _____

13. _____

14. _____

15. _____

VIII.) Your instructor may ask you to do the puzzle on the next page. It is the same as the one on your CD. You are able to do it here once or on the CD as many times as you'd like.

Across

1. to put in harm's way

3. to come between in order to solve a problem

6. having attention to detail and desire to do the very best at one's task

8. receiving the opposite of what was expected

10. complicated, detailed

11. inheritance

12. looking inward; pondering; self-examination

Down

2. inborn; existing at birth

3. hireling; motivated only by material or monetary gain; hired soldier

4. to create fear in another; to tower over; frighten

5. orderly; systematic

7. embarrassment to the point of wanting to almost die

9. active but hidden

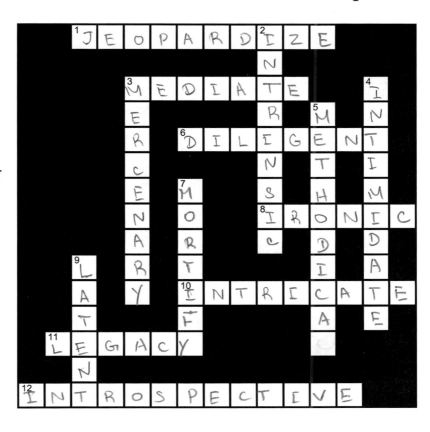

Rewrite your words

New word:		Practice writing the new word:		

Improving Essential Vocabulary and Spelling Skills

I.)　　***Reflect and Connect:*** Complete the following sentences with words that are **familiar** to you and that make sense in each sentence. You may write more than one word choice for each blank space. **<u>Do not</u> look at or study the new words yet.** Answers will vary and your instructor will discuss them with you.

mundane

niche

1. Dusting the house is a very ____general____ task, but essential if you are allergic to dust.

niche 2. Have you figured out your special ____calling____ in life?

nullify 3. Usually a person has three days in which he/she may __cancel__ a contract.

objective 4. An employer must remain ____impartial____ in deciding who would be best to hire.

obscure 5. His ideas seemed very ____indecisive____ and difficult to understand.

obsolete 6. Most typewriters are now ____out-of-date____ since the invention of the computer.

ominous 7. The dark clouds were a(n) ____dismal____ sign of a storm brewing.

pacify 8. To ____calm____ the crowd, rain checks were given for a concert the following afternoon.

persever 9. Despite difficulties, successful people learn to __sustain__ and go beyond their problems.

plagiarism 10. Jason Blair was charged with ____fraud____ for using another reporter's work without permission, and then was fired from his job as a reporter for the New York Times.

poignant 11. The movie Titanic had some very ____moving____ moments.

pragmatic 12. Some individuals are very foolish, but others are very ____logical____.

pseudonym 13. Samuel L. Clemens used the ____nick name____ Mark Twain instead of his real name.

punitive 14. The camper had to pay a large fine as ____punishing____ damages were brought against her for carelessness in starting the forest fire.

rapport 15. He showed good ____unity____ with other people, so he was hired right away.

II.) ***Study the words and definitions below.*** These words and definitions are also on the enclosed CD Rom and may be printed out as study cards. The words are broken into letter groupings for easier spelling. Also, that is followed by a common definition, and common forms of the word that you might encounter. Your instructor will pronounce the words for you or you may want to use an audio dictionary for more help.

1. **mundane (mun/dane)** 1. Belonging to the world; earthy; commonplace; ordinary; 2. boring, tedious.
2. **niche (nic/he) 1.** Suitable situation. 2. A cavity, hollow, or recess within the thickness of a wall that may be used for a statue or bust.
3. **nullify (null/i/fy)** To annul; to make void; to render invalid; to deprive of legal force or efficacy; to cancel out. Also: **nullified.**
4. **objective (ob/jec/tive)** 1. Seeing or describing something as it is; clearly stated without bias. 2. A goal; the goal.
5. **obscure (ob/sc/ure)** 1. Not easily understood; not obviously intelligible; unclear. 2. Dark; destitute of light. 3. Living in darkness. 4. Not much known or observed; retired; remote from observation. 5. Not clear, full or distinct; imperfect. 6. Not easily legible.
6. **obsolete (ob/so/lete)** No longer in active use; passed into disuse; disused; neglected.
7. **ominous (om/i/nous)** Threatening; dark; sinister; foreboding; indicating a future evil event.
8. **pacify (pa/ci/fy)** 1. To appease, as wrath or other violent passion or appetite; to calm; to still; to quiet; to allay agitation or excitement; to placate; to give in to create peace. 2. To restore peace to; to tranquilize.

9. **persevere (per/se/vere)** 1. To overcome; to continue to move forward despite difficulties. 2. To persist in any business or enterprise undertaken; to pursue steadily any design or course commenced; not to give over or abandon what is undertaken.

10. **plagiarism (pla/giar/ism)** 1. The act of purloining another person's literary works, or introducing passages from another person's writings and passing them off as one's own; literary theft. 2. Using another's work without giving proper credit to the lawful owner.

11. **poignant (poig/nant)** 1. Moving; emotionally touching. 2. Sharp; stimulating the organs of taste; as poignant sauce. 3. Pointed; keen; bitter; irritating; satirical; as poignant wit. 4. Severe; piercing; very painful or acute; as poignant pain or grief.

12. **pragmatic (prag/ma/tic)** Dealing with facts; prudent; practical.

13. **pseudonym (pseu/do/nym)** A fictitious name used by an author; an alias.

14. **punitive (pun/i/tive)** Inflicting punishment.

15. **rapport (rapp/ort)** Mutual trust; friendship.

III.) *Match the words with their definitions.* Write the letter of the correct definition before the number of the corresponding word choice.

g 1. mundane   a. unbiased

j 2. niche   b. to continue despite difficulty

m 3. nullify   c. inflicting punishment

a 4. objective   d. unclear

d 5. obscure   e. unlawful use of another's work

h 6. obsolete   f. camaraderie, friendship

k 7. ominous   g. unexciting

n 8. pacify   h. no longer in use

b 9. persevere   i. emotionally moving

e 10. plagiarism   j. suitable situation

i 11. poignant   k. threatening

l 12. pragmatic   l. prudent, wise

o 13. pseudonym   m. to cancel, make ineffective

c 14. punitive   n. to placate, to create peace

f 15. rapport   o. fictitious name

IV.) *Puzzle work.* Now try the interactive puzzle. Put the CD (that came with your workbook) into the computer, and work the puzzle. A paper copy of the puzzle is also included at the end of this chapter.

V.)   Write the correct new word in each sentence below:

niche	obscure	mundane	objective	nullify
ominous	plagiarism	obsolete	persevere	pacify
pragmatic	rapport	poignant	punitive	pseudonym

1. Dusting the house is a very ___mundane___ task, but essential if you are allergic to dust.
2. Have you figured out your special ___niche___ in life?
3. Usually a person has three days in which he/she may ___nullify___ a contract.
4. An employer must remain ___objective___ in deciding who would be best to hire.
5. His ideas seemed very ___obscure___ and difficult to understand.
6. Most typewriters are now ___obsolete___ since the invention of the computer.
7. The dark clouds were a(n) ___ominous___ sign of a storm brewing.
8. To ___pacify___ the crowd, rain checks were given for a concert the following afternoon.
9. Despite difficulties, successful people learn to ___perservere___ and go beyond their problems.
10. Jason Blair was charged with ___plagiarism___ for using another reporter's work without permission, and then was fired from his job as a reporter for the New York Times.
11. The movie Titanic had some very ___poignant___ moments.
12. Some individuals are very foolish, but others are very ___pragmatic___.
13. Samuel L. Clemens used the ___psuedonym___ Mark Twain instead of his real name.
14. The camper had to pay a large fine as ___punitive___ damages were brought against her for carelessness in starting the forest fire.
15. He showed good ___rapport___ with other people, so he was hired right away.

VI.) Are you ready to take the practice test? You may take the practice test as many times as you want to. Simply insert the CD that came with book into your computer, go to "My Computer", open the CD by clicking on it, find the Practice test folder, choose this chapter's practice test and begin. (You will need a sheet of paper to write your answers on.) When finished, turn back to this chapter and correct your test. The answers are in the same order as exercise II.

VII.) Are you ready to use the words? Write a sentence for each word.

nullify	objective	obscure	mundane	niche
pacify	persevere	plagiarism	obsolete	ominous
pseudonym	punitive	rapport	poignant	pragmatic

1. _____
_____

2. _____
_____

3. _____
_____

4. _____
_____

5. _____
_____

6. _____
_____

7. _____
_____

8. _____
_____

9. _____
_____

10. _____
_____

11. _____
_____

12. _____
_____

13. _____
_____

14. _____
_____

15. _____
_____

VIII.) Your instructor may ask you to do the puzzle on the next page. It is the same as the one on your CD. You are able to do it here once or on the CD as many times as you'd like.

Across

1. to placate; to give in, in order to create peace; appease

3. moving; emotionally touching

6. mutual trust; friendship

9. threatening; dark; sinister

10. earthy; commonplace; ordinary

12. as it is; clearly stated without bias; goal

13. to overcome; to continue to move forward despite difficulties

Down

1. using another's work without giving proper credit to the lawful owner

2. inflicting punishment

4. a fictitious name used by an author

5. to cancel out; void

7. prudent; practical; wise; savvy

8. no longer in active use

11. suitable situation

Rewrite your words

New word:		Practice writing the new word:		

Improving Essential Vocabulary and Spelling Skills

I.)   ***Reflect and Connect:*** Complete the following sentences with words that are **familiar** to you and that make sense in each sentence. You may write more than one word choice for each blank space. **Do not** look at or study the new words yet. Answers will vary and your instructor will discuss them with you.

rational   1. There is not always a ___realistic___ reason for some of the things that people do.

rationale 2. What is your ___logic___ that would support that statement?

sabotage 3. Karl tried to provoke the workers to ___damage___ the machinery.

scrutiny 4. It is wise to apply careful ___audit___ when reviewing loan documents.

secular   5. It is nearly impossible to have a truly ___civil___ government since most individuals are religious in nature.

sinister 6. Communism still has a ___corrupt___ plan to take over the world.

speculate 7. I cannot ___predict___ on what will happen in the future, but I hope for the best.

subtle   8. This hair coloring mixture promises to give ___refined___ highlights.

succint   9. The President's words were very ___short___, and he made no effort to engage the press in a "question and answer" period.

unique   10. Democracy promotes ___particular___ individuals; tyranny destroys individualism.

unscathed 11. Hector was relieved to have survived virtually ___safe___ from the accident.

vindictive 12. You cannot trust a person who has a(n) ___ruthless___ personality.

vivacious 13. Amy was the most ___cheerful___ member of the family because of her extroverted personality.

waive   14. It is usually not wise to ___reject___ your right to a jury trial.

inevitable 15. The outcome was ___undeniable___ because the evidence was overwhelmingly pointing towards his guilt.

II.) ***Study the words and definitions below.*** These words and definitions are also on the enclosed CD Rom and may be printed out as study cards. The words are broken into letter groupings for easier spelling. Also, that is followed by a common definition, and common forms of the word that you might encounter. Your instructor will pronounce the words for you or you may want to use an audio dictionary for more help.

1. **rational (ra/tion/al)** 1. Having reason or the faculty of reasoning; endowed with reason. 2. Agreeable to reason; not extravagant. 3. Acting in conformity to reason; wise; judicious; sensible.
2. **rationale (ra/tion/ale)** The underlying reasons for something being reasonable; a series of reasons attributed to a reason.
3. **sabotage (sa/bo/tage)** To deliberately cause harm.
4. **scrutiny (scru/tiny)** 1. Close search; minute inquiry; critical examination; careful examination; careful inspection. Also: **scrutinize.**
5. **secular (se/cu/lar)** Pertaining to the present world, or to things not spiritual or holy; relating to things not immediately or primarily respecting the soul, but the body; worldly; not religious.
6. **sinister (sin/is/ter)** Evil; bad; corrupt; perverse; dishonest; wicked.
7. **speculate (spec/u/late)** 1. To draw an inference based on insufficient information; theorize; sense; presume. 2. To meditate; to contemplate; to consider a subject by turning it in the mind and viewing it in its different aspects and relations. 3. In commerce, to purchase land, goods, stock or other things, with the expectation of an advance in price, and of selling the articles with a profit by means of such advance.

8. **subtle (sub/tle)** 1. Sly in design; artful; cunning; insinuating; shrewd; savvy; Cunningly devised. 2. Of a fine distinction; nice; delicate.

9. **succinct (suc/cin/ct) or (succ/in/ct)** Short; brief; concise.

10. **unique (un/i/que)** One of a kind.

11. **unscathed (un/sca/th/ed)** Not harmed.

12. **vindictive (vin/dic/tive)** Desiring revenge; spiteful.

13. **vivacious (vi/va/cious)** 1. Lively; active; sprightly in temper or conduct; energetic. 2. Having vigorous powers of life.

14. **waive (wa/ive)** To voluntarily give up legal rights; cede; relinquish.

15. **inevitable (in/ev/i/ta/ble)** Not to be avoided; that cannot be shunned; unavoidable; that admits of no escape or evasion; certain.

III.) *Match the words with their definitions.* Write the letter of the correct definition before the number of the corresponding word choice.

g. **1.** rational
m. **2.** rationale
j. **3.** sabotage
a. **4.** scrutiny
d. **5.** secular
n. **6.** sinister
h. **7.** speculate
k. **8.** subtle
b. **9.** succinct
e. **10.** unique
o. **11.** unscathed
i. **12.** vindictive
l. **13.** vivacious
c. **14.** waive
f. **15.** inevitable

a. **close inspection**
b. **brief and to the point**
c. **to give up a right**
d. **not religious**
e. **one of a kind**
f. **certain**
g. **reason(s) behind a point**
h. **theorize**
i. **desiring revenge**
j. **deliberately harm**
k. **shrewd**
l. **lively**
m. **reasonable**
n. **evil**
o. **untouched, not harmed**

IV.) *Puzzle work.* Now try the interactive puzzle. Put the CD (that came with your workbook) into the computer, and work the puzzle. A paper copy of the puzzle is also included at the end of this chapter.

V.) **Write the correct new word in each sentence below:**

sabotage	secular	rational	scrutiny	rationale
subtle	unique	sinister	succinct	speculate
vivacious	inevitable	unscathed	waive	vindictive

1. There is not always a _rational_ reason for some of the things that people do.
2. What is your _rationale_ that would support that statement?
3. Karl tried to provoke the workers to _sabotage_ the machinery.
4. It is wise to apply careful _scrutiny_ when reviewing loan documents.
5. It is nearly impossible to have a truly _secular_ government since most individuals are religious in nature.
6. Communism still has a _sinister_ plan to take over the world.
7. I cannot _speculate_ on what will happen in the future, but I hope for the best.
8. This hair coloring mixture promises to give _subtle_ highlights.
9. The President's words were very _succinct_, and he made no effort to engage the press in a "question and answer" period.
10. Democracy promotes _unique_ individuals; tyranny destroys individualism.
11. Hector was relieved to have survived virtually _unscathed_ from the accident.
12. You cannot trust a person who has a(n) _vindictive_ personality.
13. Amy was the most _vivacious_ member of the family because of her extroverted personality.
14. It is usually not wise to _waive_ your right to a jury trial.
15. The outcome was _inevitable_ because the evidence was overwhelmingly pointing towards his guilt.

VI.) **Are you ready to take the practice test?** You may take the practice test as many times as you want to. Simply insert the CD that came with book into your computer, go to "My Computer", open the CD by clicking on it, find the Practice test folder, choose this chapter's practice test and begin. (You will need a sheet of paper to write your answers on.) When finished, turn back to this chapter and correct your test. The answers are in the same order as exercise II.

VII.) Are you ready to use the words? Write a sentence for each word.

sabotage	secular	rational	rationale	scrutiny
subtle	unique	sinister	speculate	succinct
vivacious	inevitable	unscathed	vindictive	waive

1. _____

_____

2. _____

_____

3. _____

_____

4. _____

_____

5. _____

_____

6. _____

_____

7. _____

_____

8. _____

_____

9. _____

_____

10. _____

_____

11. _____

_____

12. _____

_____

13. _____

_____

14. _____

_____

15. _____

_____

VIII.) Your instructor may ask you to do the puzzle on the next page. It is the same as the one on your CD. You are able to do it here once or on the CD as many times as you'd like.

Across

3. evil; wicked

5. revengeful

6. worldly; not religious

9. to suppose; to theorize

11. deliberately destroy

12. certain; impossible to avoid

13. shrewd; of fine distinction

Down

1. one of a kind

2. to voluntarily give up

4. reasons behind a point

7. reasonable; sensible

8. lively; energetic

9. to the point; concise

10. unharmed

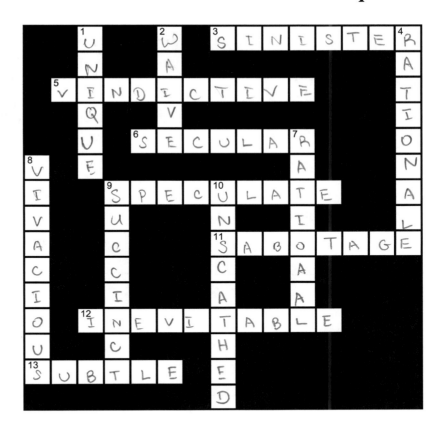

Rewrite your words

New word:	Practice writing the new word:		